M000307543

The

HEALING BASKET

A Novel

by

CLARISSA RUDOLPH-HASTINGS

Copyright © 2018 Clarissa Rudolph-Hastings
All rights reserved
First Edition

TRILOGY PUBLISHING
Tustin, Ca

First originally published by Trilogy Christian Publishing 2018

ISBN 978-1-64088-046-7 (Paperback)
ISBN 978-1-64088-047-4 (Digital)

Printed in the United States of America

DEDICATION

This book is dedicated to my parents who, by their words and example, taught me to grieve. First to my mom, who visited her dad's grave every Memorial Day. While placing flowers on his grave, she shared stories of Pablo, a man she loved very much. My mom influenced me for 29 years, but then she left me on a warm October day when she died in a fatal car accident. I will always remember the night before she passed away, when we reminisced about my childhood, and we laughed until we could barely keep our eyes open.

Her last words to me were, "Good night, and I love you, mi jita (my daughter)."

After she died, a flock of doves encircled her small adobe home for several days. They had never done that before her death, and they haven't flown over her house since those days following her funeral.

Second, I dedicate this book to my dad, who grieved with me after mom--his wife of 35 years--passed away. He became one of my best friends. My dad wasn't someone who apologized often, but I will always recall, after a heated argument--a result of his being angry at his circumstances--he regretted taking his anger out on me. I will never forget when he called me the next day to say he was sorry. He asked me how he could make it up to me.

I told him, with tears in my eyes, "You already have."

I have carried this with me because it has had a profound impact on my life, making me realize how short life is, and the importance of grace. He also died suddenly fifteen years after my mom, and a day after telling me to give kisses to "his angels," my daughters and his granddaughters. He meant the world to them and to me. For weeks after his funeral, two little bunnies peered into our home, which they had never done before. My dad always did have a sense of humor! My nine year old daughter, noticing the bunnies peering into the window, told me that her grandpa was "hoppy."

I am forever grateful to my parents because they have contributed to the woman, the mother, the wife, the writer, the teacher, and the counselor I am today. I am filled with compassion for others who grieve. Perhaps one day we will all meet again as the words in the Bible inspire us how to live life, the bunnies that visited us after my dad died remind us of the forgiveness and the humor we must seek in this world, and the birds in the air, I believe, will lead us into heaven when we die.

ACKNOWLEDGMENTS

I would like to acknowledge my husband of 29 years. I am so grateful for you fathering our amazing daughters and for inspiring one of the characters of this book. I love that you have such a great sense of humor, and an incredible heart for God. I know you pray for us, and I admire your giving our girls a glimpse of God by your example as a dad.

I would also like to acknowledge MaryClara, Susan, Paige, Melina, and Erica, all of whom call me mom. You beauties are the moon in my darkest nights! You make me convinced that God is real because of your kindness towards me and to one another. I love you all very much! No matter what happens, always stay true to yourselves and remember to let your hearts be a light to this world. You lift my spirit when it is crushed, you make me laugh when I cry, and you help me see the good in every situation. I am thankful to God for allowing me to build a relationship with each of you. Have faith always, for it is faith that gives us our spiritual health.

I further wish to acknowledge the young men in my daughters' lives, who I consider my sons: Brandon and Cesar. Keep Clara and Melina safe. They were created from your rib, near your hearts, to behold. Gaze upon their beauty and always cherish them for they are more valuable than rubies, and they will bring you good, not harm, all the days of your life.

I additionally wish to acknowledge my hometown of Las Vegas, New Mexico, where I learned about the importance of community, how to laugh at myself, and how to grieve with my family and friends. My hometown is where I had my first heartbreaks, where I went through my awkward stages and finally grew out of them, where people told me stories that scared me, where I experienced some of the saddest days of my life, and then again where I developed an appreciation for my greatest joys and accomplishments, realizing I didn't do it alone. I am incredibly thankful for the rich culture and community, where the importance of family and the beauty of our Hispanic heritage became rooted in me. I am blessed to have family and friends from such an amazing New Mexico town. You give me my greatest ideas as a writer. Yo te quiero mucho (I love you very much)!

I am blessed to have many best friends in life, and I wish to acknowledge them for they have been an answer to a constant prayer. I only asked for one friend, and God gave me many. Dina, I love that we laugh at the days to come, and you encourage me so much with your gentle words and your unfailing actions. Jennifer, your wit and thoughtfulness mean so much to me, and your loyalty is rare. Mary Francis, life is more fun and meaningful with you in it. Maria, when we get together, we talk for hours and hours…I enjoy your company so much. Sharon, I am glad our paths crossed…working with you, we made great memories--let's make some more. Diana, we connected when we lost our moms; I adored walking through the park and praying with you… I appreciate that when we get together, we pick up where we left off. You are all such awesome women….hugs!

I want to also thank the literary agent, Scott Winters, Trilogy Christian Publishing and Trinity Broadcasting Network; the editors, Bryan Norris and James Branscum; and all of the project managers, including Misty Norris, who have been involved in the production of my book. In addition, I wish to thank a special person who has been praying for me and guiding me through this process, Debby Boyd. You have such a calming spirit.

A special thank you to Joey, Safia, and Alyssa for your contribution to my photograph for this book.

Most important, I wish to thank God for teaching me how to rejoice always, even as I go through trials in life. You've showed me that love never fails, and you amaze me every morning, every day, and every evening. You are the love of my life—you constantly remind me that I am valued!

EXCERPT

"Over 10,000 American troops died that day, including my dad!" Nevaeh said as if she was trying to remember the details of that June day.

"He was awarded the Purple Heart medal for fighting at Normandy, but he would never live to receive this award. Mom and I were given this award the day of his funeral." She sadly continued.

She pulled out a small green box from her basket and opened it up. In it was his Purple Heart medal.

"You know, I was twelve years old when my dad fought at Normandy. I remember when the bus was about to leave, with the men from the 1st Infantry Division. My mom stood there, wearing a beautiful brown dress and high heels. She was built like a goddess, and I saw my dad looking at her, noticing that he loved her so much. With a handkerchief in her hand, she ran up to the bus, and my dad pushed himself out the window. He could not reach her, so the soldiers held him, pushing him further out the window. He gave her a great big kiss, a memory that never fades from my mind. The bus began to move, and the soldiers pulled him back in. My mom ran with the bus as it continued until she could no longer chase it. The last thing I remember is my mom standing there alone, bringing the handkerchief to her face as she composed herself. She recognized my dad's cologne on the handkerchief and at that moment, she intuitively realized she had just kissed him good-bye, forever."

CHAPTER

1

Memories of the righteous are a blessing.

I will remember you. I will see you in my mind. I will hear your voice. I will feel you in my heart. Always, I will remember you.

When I was a little girl, I used to visit an older, Hispanic woman down the road from my childhood home. For a newcomer to New Mexico, imagine an old adobe home, built by the Spaniards in the mid 18th Century whose buildings were influenced by the Pueblo Indian tribes. It was a yellow house, having a flat roof and small windows. At one time, the house had dirt floors, and an outhouse was used as a latrine, but it was modernized with wood floors and indoor plumbing with a bathroom the size of a walk-in closet. Her home was a small humble abode, warmed in the winter with wood stoves, by which this kindhearted woman also cooked the best meals I've ever tasted. The house often smelled of fresh baked bread, pies, and cakes, an aroma no one ever wants to forget. The old wood stove made the senses of your nose inhale vehemently, like a ravenous soldier who had not tasted home cooking since being on deployment for many months. Enjoying the taste of food, I remember masking my impatience as she would take the bread out of the oven and put the loaves on a cutting board. After waiting five minutes for the bread to cool down, she would cut a piece for me, adding a dab of butter, which melted quickly on the steamy hot bun. Then she would look at my face, noticing my big brown eyes, and I would smile with approval, salivating with anticipation. It was worth the wait…the bread tasted so good as I chewed it slowly, one piece at a time.

After eating the fresh baked bread, I watched her short, thin stature as she worked around the kitchen, almost gliding across the floor; her arms were strong for her tasks. Her hair was short and dark, as dark as a black stallion and just as thick. I noticed gray hairs beginning to show, but they were neatly brushed back. Her piercing eyes were dark brown like the Mona Lisa and almond-shaped. She had incredibly high cheekbones, making her look noble. Having thin lips, she accentuated them with a light shade of lipstick. Her clothes were from an era before my time. She wore straight long skirts and long-sleeved button shirts. Her shoes had a slight heel and looked like character shoes that we would see in the ballet stores when we shopped in the city. As she baked, she often hummed songs from another time, which I learned about in school during my history lessons. She liked Latin music and sometimes moved her body like a sultry washing machine. She made me smile because I imagined her free spirit filling the house with happiness and continuous gratitude.

Together, Nevaeh, a glorious name given to her by her grandmother, and I would clean the kitchen. She would wash the pots and pans and wipe down the counters and the table where there were crumbs from the bread. I was given the task of drying the dishes with an old clean rag, a part of a bath towel. She was the cleanest woman I knew. Her kitchen floors were covered with shiny plastic floor mats, and I never saw one single stain, a piece of lint or any dirt on them. As we labored together on this particular day, she looked out the window, which was right in front of the sink, and noticed the snow falling from her big, strong oak tree. At first, she said that God knows us by our names and did not want us to live in fear. She told me that she had visited New England one winter, staying with her dad's family. Her visit evoked a trepidation about the snow. She had not really thought about the damage a heavy snowfall frozen on top of a tree could cause until she drove through the forests of New Hampshire. She said while her vehicle slowly moved from one group of trees to another, she noticed the branches of these tall saplings hanging down. The snow would every once in a while plummet in front of her car, and she would hear a sound like a loud cymbal in a band that could not be avoided. She was afraid that the car would be smashed by the heavy snow falling from the trees, but it never was. When she returned home from New Hampshire, she became more aware of the snow tumbling from the winter branches of the old oak tree outside her window, and she began realizing that the weight of frozen ice could be dangerous. Once again, this triggered apprehension, making her afraid of the sleet hitting her house. She would imagine the layers of ice on her flat roof top and knew it was just a matter of time until the heaviness would cause it to cave in. I wondered what she meant, as I began to imagine the ceilings in every room bending inward from the weight of the snow. This really scared me.

"Nevaeh," I asked, "I don't really understand. Is the falling snow really going to come into your house? I think the roof is stronger than the snow."

She smiled, almost laughing.

"My sweet child," she said, "Sometimes we need to take captive our thoughts because if we don't, we worry constantly. I was thinking in my head that if the snow hit the car hard when I was in New Hampshire, I might have an accident. You see, my dear, New Hampshire was like a far-off land to me. In a distant place, where everything seems strange to you, you notice things you never were afraid of in your homeland. It's like when Jesus, after the crucifixion, appeared to his disciples, and they were afraid of him because they didn't immediately recognize him, so he had to remind them that he was Jesus. I mean, the disciples scattered when Jesus was being beaten, and Peter even denied knowing Jesus three times out of fear. When Jesus rose from the dead, he united with them again, and at first, they were frightened. Later, however, when they could see Jesus, hear his voice and even Thomas had to touch the wounds on his hands to believe it was really him, it was then that they became fearless."

She continued. "There is a security with our comfortable belief system, but then something extraordinary happens, and we don't even recognize it as absolutely amazing. Things somehow seem different, so our certainty is questioned. Life is like the vicious snow storms all around us, similar to the beatings that Jesus endured, so our minds drift and we forget about the Creator and start to think about what could happen—if only this or that happens—focusing on the power of the creation. We begin to imagine that there is more strength in nature while in our minds God becomes weaker and smaller. We can hear the wind howling through the night, and as the falling ice begins pounding on the roof, it triggers thoughts of the scary forests in New Hampshire, which are actually quite beautiful. The snow could one day hit the house hard enough to cave into the roof or break branches, eventually shattering windows, but we only let our minds drift when we are away from what we've been taught, like when the disciples were away from Jesus for a short time after he was crucified. They forgot all the miracles they had witnessed and stopped believing that he is the Messiah. We are the same way. We take for granted that we are protected from the things that cause fear in a remote place. We realize these fears lie deep within us like an evil spirit locked in a box. When terror confronts us, we understand that we must let it go, so we can be free from dread. When I looked outside my window after coming home from New Hampshire, I noticed the snow falling, as if I were a small insecure child noticing a scary spider or a large snake for the first time. It occurred to me that while in New Hampshire, I did not need to fear what was in front of me all of my life. It just never occurred to me that I could be affected in my home by the things that caused me stress outside of here. You see, I missed the beauty of the snow falling in New Hampshire because I was focused on being terrified of skidding off the road as a result of being hit by the snow, but I have always enjoyed watching it in front of my window at home, even during the stormy weather. The disciples stopped believing in the influence of Jesus and they went to remote places that made them more afraid because of their skewed thoughts. I'm glad in all my years of living here I didn't worry about the snow storms that violently tried to enter my house, thinking they could terrify my life. They never have scared me, until I left my home. If I had lived in constant fear all the years I have resided here, I might have never enjoyed the beauty of New Mexico. Instead, I would have existed in panic mode, and this is punishment for our souls. I didn't really enjoy my time in New Hampshire. Fear overtook my spirit for the brief time I visited New England, but now that I am home, I am no longer afraid. I am so grateful for the scriptures because God tells us that even when we walk in the darkest valley, we are to fear no evil because God is with us. When Jesus returned to the disciples after his death, and after they recognized him, they were motivated by love, and so they went back to what they were taught by Jesus and what they believed. I understand now that anxiety will leave my mind when I notice I am not alone. When I look for God and *see* Jesus, I am not afraid. In New Hampshire, I was blinded by fear. Now I see clearly. I believe in the power of God, not in the what if's. Do you understand?"

"Yes," I said with my eyes as big as the round bread pans I was drying, thinking about the snow caving in, as I looked up at the roof.

I really had no clue what she was saying to me, although I was trying to understand. I just didn't want her to think I was dumb. I was eleven years old, an honor student and quite gifted. Everyone said I was smart. I couldn't let Nevaeh know I didn't have the slightest idea what she was talking about. She did this to me sometimes, but I didn't mind because she was so wise. I thought that maybe I was not seeing something, although I understood feeling frightened about things in life. I wasn't afraid of snow, however. In fact, I enjoyed playing in the snow. I had never even thought of it making the roof cave in. My uncles were excellent roofers; so of course, I didn't fear snow causing damage on the roof. They had built my house. I was safe, but I wasn't sure about the evil spirits. I was hoping they didn't exist.

Note to self: "Ask one of my uncles to check Nevaeh's roof, and tell mom to call Pastor Salas to bless this house."

Nevaeh looked around the kitchen, took the drying towel out of my hand, and hung it near the wood stove. She took some lotion from the counter, asked for my hands and rubbed some of the lotion on them. She walked into the living room, right next to the kitchen, and I followed her. I looked around, not wanting to miss a thing. I observed the painting, which hung in the kitchen as you entered the living room. It was a depiction of the *Last Supper*. Every Hispanic family had such a painting. I must have seen it one thousand times in various homes, but I never really noticed the details. This time it kind of scared me, but I did not have to be troubled, I thought. It was like the snow on the old oak tree. It had always been there, and I didn't want to miss its beauty. I secretly told the evil spirits to flee from me so I could be free from feeling uneasy. Gosh, Nevaeh really made me think! Now I'm petrified of a painting I have been exposed to all of my life, or maybe I hadn't *seen* it. I wasn't going to let fear come between the picture and me. I gazed at the painting again. This time I admired the hues of color and the texture. Besides, Jesus was in the middle of the picture. He kept me shielded because I remember Nevaeh saying he knows me by my name. I think I knew what Nevaeh was talking about this time, but I still wasn't one hundred percent sure. Maybe one day I would be certain.

Nevaeh and I went straight to the record player. She had many records, but I didn't like most of them. We lived in the small town of Agua de Vida, which meant "Water of Life," in northern New Mexico. Many of the local people were Hispanic. My Uncle Juan Jose Jimenez, who was a second generation Mexican American, had many arguments with family members about the name "Hispanic." Uncle Se, which is what all the nieces and nephews called him, referred to himself as "Chicano." I didn't quite understand the difference between "Hispanic" and "Chicano" because we all spoke English and Spanish, and we had European ancestry, but if you called my Uncle Se Hispanic or my Hispanic uncles Mexican American, there would be arguing for hours. I considered myself Hiscana, half Hispanic and half Chicana.

I would sometimes yell in my head, "Can't we just all get along! Let's just call ourselves Hiscana!!"

I never dared said it out loud. It would cause more arguing, and my family was loud. I would just cover my ears and pretend I couldn't hear them. They were ridiculous sometimes. This is why I spent as much time away from them and with Nevaeh every other weekend.

Nevaeh had many albums and listened to Nino de Murcio, Freddy Fender, and Linda Ronstadt, but I preferred the Bee Gees. I gave her a record from *Saturday Night Fever* for Christmas, and she said she would only play it when I visited. She liked the song *More Than a Woman.* I thought it was the lamest song on the album. This album was a big hit to teenagers, and I only listened to it because I had older siblings who liked to dance. Everyone wanted to dress like John Travolta, and he was good looking. I liked his smile and the fact that he was Italian. If I married him, my uncles would have another argument on their hands. What would our children be considered if I married John Travolta? Part Italian, part Chicana, and part Hispanic.

"Histaliana!" I thought. "I kind of like it!"

When she put the needle on the album and it began to play, I would sing the lyrics with Nevaeh, pretending to be the woman in John Travolta's arms. I always imagined Nevaeh was John Travolta, but I never told her that because she would think I was loca (crazy), so I kept it to myself. Our favorite part was at the beginning of the song.

Dancing, we sang even louder, "Here in your arms I found my paradise, my only chance for happiness and if I lose you now I think I would die. Say you'll always be my baby. We could make forever just a minute at a time. More than a woman, more than a woman to me, more than a woman, more than a woman to me."

A year ago, I had begged my parents to take me to the drive-in theater to see the movie, but they said no. My mom and dad thought it was a sex crazed teen movie, but I thought it was a dance movie. I pretended to dance with John Travolta, or JT, who looked foxy in that white suit, all the time in my room. He was so much older than me, but no one could know how deeply I felt for this older man. It was something everyone would tease me about if they knew, so I kept my crush on John Travolta to myself. One day our age difference wouldn't matter. Besides, even though I longed to meet him and marry him one day, I knew our paths would probably never cross. Or maybe they would? I could always wish, right? Neveah would tell me not to idolize John Travolta.

"If we idolize people, they always disappoint us. Jesus should be the one we should aspire to be like and love the most." Nevaeh would tell me every time I would talk about JT.

She would say I would never be disheartened if I put JC, Jesus Christ, over JT. As usual, she was right. Life teaches us how much we need JC, who should always be in the center of our pictures. Nevaeh twirled me around as the song came to a close, and I fell to the ground.

"Groovy oovy!" I shouted.

We laughed. Nevaeh stopped the record player.

"It is getting late, my little friend. I promised your mom I would only keep you for a couple hours, and it has been over that, I'm sure. I will send some bread home with you."

Nevaeh walked to the table where she placed several loaves of bread in a recycled plastic bag.

When I first started visiting Nevaeh, my mom would tell me that I must never take advantage of her and should not only visit her for food, but I should also get to know her. I took my mom's advice, and Nevaeh had become one of my best friends. Being gifted and slightly overweight, I was considered quite odd in my community. I had a difficult time relating to children my own age. I could relate better to older people. I had more in common with them. I liked to hear about politics, gardening, and the Farmer's Almanac. Even though I was in fifth grade, my friend Sarah and I had third graders at school who followed us everywhere we went when they got the chance. Sometimes we made them carry our books, but then we would sit them down and read to them. Sarah was my one and only fifth grade best friend, and would ride the bus with me to school 30 miles away. Her full name was Sarah Marie Garcia, a name meaning "princess." We both had Biblical names. Mine was Mary Grace Martinez, which Neveah told me meant "gift of God." Sarah and I lived close to each other but not within walking distance. We didn't see each other very often after school hours, and we always had chores to do, like cleaning the chicken coop, collecting eggs, and helping with the gardening in the summer and fall, or shoveling snow in the winter. My social life was next to nothing, but I didn't mind. I had Nevaeh, who lived within walking distance to me.

After Nevaeh packed up some bread, she took out some of her choke cherry jelly, and frozen green chili. I gave her a long hug. She always smelled so good.

"Good-bye, Mary Grace. I will see you in two weeks," Nevaeh said. "Have your mom call me when you get home."

"Okay. Thank you. See you soon," I said as I bundled up and walked out the front door.

I fearlessly passed the old oak tree. The snow was no longer falling from the tree. The temperature had fallen, and everything stood frozen.

CHAPTER

2

In deep waters, God is with us, so we are not dismayed.

*I could not feel my frozen toes in the winter
snow, but even with the freezing temperatures,
I did not wish to focus on what was behind
me. It had passed. I could not imagine what
was in my future. It wasn't here yet. I only
saw what was immediately in front of me.*

"Mary Grace!" Sarah shouted.

My best friend, mi amiga! Her hair was like a goddess, long, dark, and wavy. Her skin was like the night. She had beautiful thick lips and eyes like her Native American grandmother. She and her mother lived with her grandmother in one of the oldest adobe homes in our hometown. Her father had died in a beer brawl in a small tavern nearby. He had been stabbed to death. Sarah did not talk about him, perhaps she did not remember much about him, but she was happy go lucky. Nothing ever seemed to bother her.

"I had such a great Christmas," she said sitting next to me on the bus.

"What did you do?" I asked.

"My uncle brought us this beautiful large Christmas tree that he cut from his property. We stringed popcorn and made decorations. I made the star out of aluminum foil and buttons. I got a Barbie doll, Snoopy bubble bath, and these mittens and the hat and scarf that I'm wearing today. We baked pies and cooked the turkey that ate my shoe string last summer. There was no shoe string in that turkey. I wonder where it went, but we ate good food. My mom said we were very blessed this year."

Yes, I thought. We are very blessed. We didn't get many gifts. There wasn't a lot of money to spend on decorations and presents. We were so grateful, however, for what we did receive. We depended on one another and celebrated the Holy Days, as Nevaeh used to call them. It didn't matter how much you had. What mattered were the blessings in our lives. We were proud people and didn't take our blessing for granted. Dios, our God, always took care of us, and we had all we needed.

"How was your Christmas, Mary Grace?" Sarah asked.

"It was fun. I saw Nevaeh, and we baked bread. My mom's family stayed with us for two weeks. I had all my cousins staying in my room. We laughed and stayed up until the sun came out. We made a snowman as big as Santa Claus and put my uncle's gloves on it. It had big buttons for eyes, a carrot for a nose, and we decorated its mouth with candy. We borrowed my grandpa's hat and placed it on the snowman's head. It was a great Christmas." I said.

As we drove to school in the bus, laughing and thinking of the great Christmas we had, there were moments of silence. We began listening to the two older boys behind us talking about a girl who had been arrested over the break. They said something about an accidental shooting. Someone was shot and killed. I felt alarmed, like the kind of fear Nevaeh was talking about. I had just entered a "foreign land." I didn't feel safe. I kept thinking about the picture of Jesus and his disciples. I remembered the colors in the picture, and the love of JC. Love equals Jesus. I'm protected. I got it! Jesus, who is love, drives out the demons around us, so I didn't have to be scared. I clung on to God and looked out the window at the snow. Funny how Jesus was the first one I could think about at a time like this. John Travolta could not keep me from being fearful. Only Jesus could.

When we arrived at school, we were told to go straight to class. Everyone seemed very quiet. Even though I felt nervous, I kept thinking about what Neveah had said about walking through a dark valley with God, who drove out frightening thoughts. I had to let it go, to keep my soul focused on being calm and enjoying my day at school, to get rid of anything that interfered with feeling brave, so I thought about the Holy days that we had celebrated. I focused on what I believed to be true, and I meditated on the fact that Jesus was the center of my life. Nothing could possibly ruin this day.

Mrs. Greene, my fifth grade teacher who was usually very upbeat, seemed rather serious. As we hung our jackets and sat in our desks, she stood in front of the room, and she was thinking intently.

"Students," she stated carefully, I have some very sad news. "As you might have noticed, Hope is not here today."

I looked back to my right. Hope was rarely in class. I didn't notice she was gone. It wasn't unusual. She was the loner girl, who smelled really bad. Her hair was blonde and eyes blue. She was the "gringa" in class. Sarah and I thought she was half Caucasian and half Hispanic, but we weren't sure. Her dad was definitely not Hispanic and not from this area. He moved into the house on the hill with his wife, who I had only seen in a picture. She looked like a beautiful painting, which she had posed in, along with their older daughter. Hope carried that picture with her like a prize, even though it was becoming worn. They sometimes attended church but left right after, socializing with just a few people. My parents said that they had moved to our small town from the city and were looking to escape from the hustle and bustle of Chicago. Sarah and I befriended Hope, but she missed school frequently. Her hair was always in her face and it was usually greasy and straight. She wore the same clothes day after day, and although we suspected she didn't have a lot of food at home due to her fragile, thin frame, she rarely ate at school, either. Her mom died suddenly during Hope's birth, and Hope told me she sometimes felt responsible, although she was just a baby. My mom felt badly that a little girl had to carry the burden of having no woman in her life--and then for her to think that she was responsible for her mom's death was not what any child should convey within herself. In our community, most women had their babies at home. There were no hospitals close by. In fact, Nevaeh told me she came back to our home town to have her daughter, Lily. Her husband had been stationed at White Sands Missile Range in New Mexico when she became pregnant, and she traveled over four hours by bus, just a few weeks before she delivered Lily. It was rare that someone died having their baby, but I remember Hope telling me that her mom had died giving birth to her. She once confided in me and secretly wished she had died too. I sorrowfully thought about this at school as our teacher continued to speak. I also wondered what Mrs. Greene was going to tell us and knew it had something to do with what we had heard on the bus earlier that morning.

"She will not be back," she continued. "As you may have heard, her older sister was arrested over the Holidays. Hope is okay and will be going away to live with another family. I don't know the details, but please keep them in your prayers."

I couldn't think about anything else for the rest of the day. During lunch, Sarah and I were both somber. We thought that we could have done something to help Hope. We should have been stronger and tried to figure out a way to go to her house and comfort her. The problem was, she was not living in her house anymore. She must have felt so alone and now both of her parents were dead. Some of our fellow students were saying that the older sister accidentally shot the dad. How could something so tragic happen? It wasn't unusual for us to have guns. We were all taught how to use them at a young age. I knew how to shoot a rifle and had gone hunting with my dad, uncles and cousins just last fall, when I turned eleven. However, I never even heard of anyone who had shot another human being, especially in our small town. Sarah and I, for the first time in our lives, grieved for someone our own age. We grieved because Hope was alone, going through all of this. The pain we felt penetrated deep into our hearts.

After school, as the bus traveled toward our homes, there was silence. No one said a word. When something happened in our town to one person or family, it affected us all.

"Mary Grace," Sarah whispered.

I looked at her. For the first time, my best friend, who seemed joyful at all times, wiped the tears that fell from her eyes.

"I know how she feels, Mary Grace. I know," she said quietly.

I took my arms and wrapped them around her. We sat in the bus hugging for several minutes, not saying a word. We didn't have to speak. We had been educated today like no other day. We had lost Hope that day. I looked outside. I did not see any snow falling from the trees, or perhaps I did not notice the fear I felt. Sometimes fear is before us, and we don't notice it. I just hugged my best friend who cried. Sadness had brought us together that day. Like the weather around us, we could feel the cold breeze that surrounded our community. Mother Nature had made herself known.

CHAPTER

3

God works out everything for the good of those who love him.

I can feel pain for the first time in my life. I can see you in my dreams, your frail body, your blue eyes, and your blonde hair. I can see your face crying out to me. I can hear your voice in my head. Your name is Hope. I do not know if you exist anymore, or if you are within the depth of my pain, my anguish, and my grief, which are masking you. We will meet again someday. I promise.

I didn't know what else to do when I arrived home. I had to see Nevaeh. I didn't usually visit her after school. I only went over during some weekends. I had to go over this day. She was the only person who could help me understand this anguish. On most days, we would talk about her garden, and I fondly have memories of the fresh vegetables she would wash for me to take home to my family in the summer months. I learned so much from her, listening to stories about the Bible, the depression, politics, her daughter, and her grandchildren, who she adored.

On this gloomy afternoon, when my heart ached like never before, I stood at her door for a long time knocking. I could see her wiping tears from her eyes through the front window panes. Her hair was not neatly in a bun, but it was straight, and I could see her gray hairs tangled like she had not combed it. She was wearing jeans and an old sweatshirt, with slippers on her feet. Her appearance was not put together this day. She looked hideous, like a vieja, an old lady, but I didn't care. I needed her to be there for me. I needed my best friend to put her arms around me like I had done for Sarah. She finally opened the door, and stillness filled the air. I wondered if this day had been planned, somehow, and we were meant to feel sad, together. We were both hurting like a fresh cut on your skin, when you suddenly notice the pain of an open wound, and the pain is delayed until you see blood everywhere.

I began sobbing like a baby when she opened the door. I could tell, as this visit was unexpected, she was reluctant to invite me in. She let me enter her house, however, and together, we slowly walked across the old wood floors. It did not smell of fresh baked bread this day, there were no vegetables waiting for me to take home in the cold of winter. I only saw a large basket on her coffee table, opened up. Inside, I could see pictures, cards, pressed lilies, an aged teddy bear, and a handkerchief with fading red lipstick.

She began to tell me that she never wanted me to see her this way. She was always joyful in our past meetings, but this was a day of melancholy.

"What is making *you* cry, my young friend?" She asked seemingly concerned.

"Hope's sister accidentally shot their dad," I began telling her.

"I know, Mary Grace. I think everyone has heard the sad news." She said, trying to smile, but I could see she was trying to conceal the tears that were in her eyes.

"Nevaeh," I asked, "Why are you crying?"

"There is much grief today," she replied.

She just looked at me as tears welled up in both of our eyes. She was silent for several minutes, which seemed like a long time in my estimation.

"Why are you so down?" I asked, concerned that Nevaeh, who had always been upbeat, was as upset as me. "Please tell me. I bet it would help both of us."

She looked at me, with a half-smile and began to unenthusiastically tell me that on that day, twenty years before, she had lost her mom, the one person who had loved her more than life itself. She didn't want to share her depressing story, as she could see I was upset.

"Please continue, Nevaeh." I begged.

"I will only resume to tell you what all this means, the basket, the memories in the basket, if you want me to, but you may not fully understand," she carefully continued.

"We are both tearful," I started. "Tell me why you are blue, and I will tell you about my sorrow. That is what friends are for, right?"

I wanted her to explain. I needed for her to share her story. I told her how important it was that she told me about the basket, so she gave in and began sharing the memories she had been crying about. She said she had many memories of her mom around her home, like that mirror in her front room that had been passed down for several generations, an old bookcase that her dad had made for her mom before they were married, the dining room table with chairs that were broken but had been glued together, a beautiful wedding picture of her parents, smiles from long ago, and the china in her cabinet that her mom gave to her weeks before she died, as if she knew she would be leaving soon. Her dad had been killed in World War II when she was about my age, a little older, only 12 years old. After her dad passed away her mom had raised her, alone, opening a small café to support them. Nevaeh loved baking because it reminded her of their café.

She then detailed the story of her mom dying tragically in a car accident as she traveled through our small town. A drunk driver, who was driving a big truck, ran a red light, t-boned her mom's car, and her mom died instantaneously. As I saw the tears in her eyes, I grabbed her hand. It was cold. I thought the tears would stop by my gesture, but they continued to fall. I tried to say something encouraging, thinking that I would see the tears in her eyes cease from falling down her cheeks, that I could somehow fix this moment, but the tears came out anyway. She reached out to me that day, hugging me tightly. I surrendered my valor and cried with her. I had been exposed to the same kind of pain earlier that day.

We went through the basket, the healing basket, as she referred to it. Then she shared a story about the dry lilies, lilies that her mom had given her when she completed high school. They had been carefully pressed and preserved. No one in her family had ever completed high school before, but the lilies represented to her a momentous occasion. Her mom handed her these lilies as she walked down the stairs from the stage, after receiving her diploma. She told me that her mom smiled bigger than any of the other parents, and she could still remember the pounding of her heart as she embraced her mom.

Nevaeh then went back in time, all the way to the year when she was about to turn six years old. It was 1938. The year had started with the 24th Rose Bowl, where California beat Alabama, 14-0. Her parents did not have television, so her mom and dad, along with their many brothers and sisters, 22 between the two families, to be exact, listened to the game on an old transistor radio. Her dad was on a furlough from the United States Army. Nevaeh was expected to be born on the last day of March, but her mom went into labor one week earlier than expected, on March 23rd. Between January and Nevaeh's sixth birthday, many historical events occurred. On February 4th, Hitler seized control of Germany, while, on that same day, Disney's *Snow White and the Seven Dwarfs* was officially released. She didn't know what was happening in Germany, but she definitely was so excited about the Disney movie being released. She and her mom would have to travel over 1,200 miles just to watch it, in California. She was given an early birthday gift from her dad, two tickets to watch the movie. It was unheard of to get tickets before a movie, but somehow her dad did it. She didn't know how he got those tickets, but he let her mom take her to see it, since they only had two tickets. I wondered why something so terrible happened in Germany while one of the greatest movies of all time could have been released on the same day. In 1938, there were rumors about Adolf Hitler, but no one could foresee the atrocities this mastermind caused in the course of history through his crimes to humanity. Nevaeh told me that in history, if you knew then what you know now, it would be changed, but it's hardly ever different. We mostly learn from the pain, and some people repeat it. Nevaeh then told me that her dad had died during the invasion of Normandy on June 6, 1944, also known as D-day.

"Over 10,000 American troops died that day, including my dad!" Nevaeh said as if she was trying to remember the details of that June day.

"He was awarded the Purple Heart medal for fighting at Normandy, but he would never live to receive this award. Mom and I were given this award the day of his funeral." She sadly continued.

She pulled out a small green box from her basket and opened it up. In it was his Purple Heart medal.

"You know, I was twelve years old when my dad fought at Normandy. I remember when the bus was about to leave, with the men from 1st Infantry Division. My mom stood there, wearing a beautiful brown dress and high heels. She was built like a goddess, and I saw my dad looking at her, noticing that he loved her so much. With a handkerchief in her hand, she ran up to the bus, and my dad pushed himself out the window. He could not reach her, so the soldiers held him, pushing him further out the window. He gave her a great big kiss, a memory that never fades from my mind. The bus began to move, and the soldiers pulled him back in. My mom ran with the bus as it continued until she could no longer chase it. The last thing I remember is my mom standing there alone, bringing the handkerchief to her face as she composed herself. She recognized my dad's cologne on the handkerchief and at that moment, she intuitively realized she had just kissed him good-bye, forever."

Nevaeh paused, but only for a second and continued telling the story, "My mom turned to me. She tried holding back the tears, but I could see them coming."

"Your dad is a brave soldier. No matter what happens, remember his bravery, always, Nevaeh!" She said to me, firmly.

"Then she knelt beside me and hugged me. I began to cry because I felt something wasn't quite right." Nevaeh continued speaking.

She pulled out a picture from her healing basket. She showed me pictures of a family, her family, posing in front of an army base. *I* saw a handsome young man in a military uniform, a nicely dressed woman holding his arm, and a little girl between them. *She* saw herself, a grieving child, and her dad and mom, who she missed every day. She took the teddy bear and placed it near her heart, telling me how her dad had won it for her at an amusement park, and her mom had kept it stored in a cedar chest, to be given to her when she became a mother herself. Tears flowed down her cheeks again as she whispered that her mom had not known her granddaughter or great grandchildren.

"When we moved to San Diego, California to be close to my dad, I used to sing to the troops." She said.

"Shirley Temple was well-known back then, and my mom would curl my hair just like her!" Nevaeh exclaimed.

She would sing a song called *I'm a Big Girl Now.*

Nevaeh stood up and sang it to me with a big old smile on her face, even as she allowed the tears down her cheeks. "I'm a big girl now. I'm a big girl now. I want to be treated like a big girl now. When daddy says a certain joke that isn't fair. I'm tired of going to movies with my Uncle Tim. I'm tired of going to picnics with my old Aunt Min. I want to sing to all the troops at Central Park. I want to travel across the world with mom and dad. I'm a big girl now!"

I clapped and was so impressed with Nevaeh's vocals.

"Wow Nevaeh! I didn't know you could sing," I said fervently.

Nevaeh just sat down, dazed, staring into nowhere. She seemed to almost forget that I was there.

"Nevaeh?" I asked. "Are you okay?"

She looked at me, but with a blank look on her face.

"I stopped singing after my dad died." She said.

Nevaeh pulled out a note that her dad had written to her mom. It was barely readable, but Nevaeh had memorized what was on the note.

"To my beautiful bride," she began. "You are the rose of Sharon, and the lily of the valleys. As the lily among thorns, so is my love among the daughters. (Song of Solomon 2:1-2). You are the most beautiful flower I have ever laid my eyes upon, more beautiful than a rose or any other flower in existence today. My heart beats like a drum when I think about you. Forever your husband!"

"My daughter's name is Lily," she said with a smile on her face, wiping the tears off her face.

"I love the image this letter gives me. Try to imagine different kinds of flowers in a field, roses, orchids, poppies, apple blossoms, pincushions, and geraniums but the lilies stand out as the most beautiful. They grow to be some of the strongest flowers of them all." She said confidently.

She changed her demeanor, almost sounding like a teacher. "Did you know the lily is a symbol for purity and refined beauty? True lilies are never dormant, and they even have medicinal purposes. Some are used to relieve heart disease, which shows just how amazing they are, while others diffuse a sweet honey perfume, so they smell so good."

Looking down at the picture, she continued, "My dad saw my mom's heart, and he loved the depth of her being. I sometimes wonder if God took him young just so that I would always remember their love as ideal. Maybe God used this tragedy so I would *see* my own daughter as the lily that stands out, not with a critical spirit. We must observe those precious messages that God sends us in the darkness of our despair. Otherwise, we lose hope."

I didn't want to lose hope. It was ironic to me how I learned about my friend Hope on this very day, and now Nevaeh was talking about losing hope. I felt despair today, so I wanted to find God's message in this dark day. I didn't understand why tragedy occurred. I just wanted to find the significance that God had for me in spite of the gloom that seemed to drown me. What was God trying to teach me?

"I want hope back, like hot cocoa, with marshmallows, on a cold winter day. Please, Nevaeh, is there a scripture you can share about hope?" I asked.

Nevaeh often read scriptures to me. She said the words in the Bible were the bread of life.

She looked at me, as though she were reading the feelings in my eager eyes. She picked up her Bible from the end table and opened it up.

With a deep breath, Nevaeh quoted scripture, "Hebrews 6:19 says, 'Which hope we have as an anchor of the soul, both sure and steadfast, and which entereth into that within the veil.'"

"What does this mean?" I asked. "I don't understand what that means."

"Well, let me see how to explain it." Nevaeh said, as she looked at my anxious face.

"Let me first say that sometimes we can read the scriptures many times, and we are left with a new understanding. It's not that the scriptures change meaning; we are the ones who change. So, let me begin by saying this world is like a great big ocean. Historically, while at sea, those in the navy would use an anchor to hold their ship when it was a clear day, or to keep them from going under during storms and harsh waves. Hope is like that anchor. It is unseen, but we know it is there. It keeps us from drowning in our sorrow, in our pain, and in our sad days. If we let him, God is the captain of our ship, and we are his ship mates. Like a veil that shields the face of a bride, he will protect us from the storms, if we don't give up our hope. We are anchored by hope. We are safe, even when we fear what we cannot understand. We must rely on hope. It will not disappoint us." She looked at me, to make sure I was following what she was saying.

I was very honest this time, "I think I understand, Nevaeh. Even though we can't see it, we must not give up on hope because God is the one anchoring us and keeping us above the water, like a bride being protected by her groom?"

She hugged me tightly, giggling with excitement, and said, "Yes, that is exactly what it means my little friend! This is what it means to you, and this is what it means to me! God is our hope! I love you so much!"

"I love you too, and thank you for making me feel better." I said as she separated herself from me, so she could look at my face, making sure I was okay to walk home.

"You have school tomorrow, and it is getting late. Can I make you a sandwich to go?" She asked.

I was so hungry and couldn't turn down one of Nevaeh's tuna sandwiches. As she made it, I asked her to sing for me, *I'm a Big Girl Now!* We danced a little, and I realized hope had returned to me, and to Nevaeh because she was singing the song she used to sing to the soldiers, something she hadn't done since her dad had died. I was no longer sad. Nevaeh had made me happy. She could reveal a happy spirit in a dark day, even in the midst of a storm.

Nevaeh packed me a sandwich, some celery sticks, and some milk. I walked home, thinking about the scripture of hope. I couldn't see hope, but I knew hope was my anchor, so I could remain steadfast and sure that I had not lost hope. God was in charge of my ship. He would never let the storms overtake me. Instead of losing hope, I had gained courage.

CHAPTER

4

The Lord is my helper, I will not live in fear.

*I cannot see the anchor of hope, but I know
it is with me. My captain is God, and
in this ship, which is my safe haven, are
my family and friends. We will make it
through the storms. I am sure of this!*

When I arrived home, my mom was worried about me.

"Where have you been, little lady?" She asked.

Scared like a doe in the woods, I looked up at my mom, my eyes wide open. I didn't want to be in trouble, but I had an idea. I had made my mom worry.

"I was at Nevaeh's." I replied.

"I called everyone I could think of, except Nevaeh, because you never go see her after school. You should always let me know where you go. I was afraid something had happened to you!" She said, seeming rather relieved but angry at the same time.

"I heard some bad news about Hope today, mom, and Nevaeh made me feel better. Look, she even made me a sandwich!" I said.

"I know. I'm so sorry about Hope. Everyone has been affected." She paused. "It's a good thing that you have a sandwich to eat because I was going to have to dig into the cupboard and make you something. Your brothers ate your portion of food this evening, so I'm glad you have something to eat, thanks to Nevaeh."

I sat down at the kitchen table and took the sandwich out of the plastic bag. I was very hungry. While I ate the sandwich, I talked to my mom about Hope and what I had heard. She reminded me of a picture we had made using our handprints a few years ago in school.

"You, Sarah, and Hope had started making handprints in third grade, for Thanksgiving. It was supposed to have been a turkey, but then some boys put their handprints on it too. You girls were so mad at the boys because they ruined your picture." She said.

"Do you remember I had to come by the principal's office? You girls took the paint and threw it on the boy's clothes. I was talking to Sarah's mom, and I remember Hope's dad walking into the school. He was a mechanic, so his hands were full of oil. We tried shaking his hand, but he just gave us a stern look and grabbed Hope's arm, without even meeting with the principal. Hope stayed out of school for a week after that." My mom reminded me.

"Do you still have that picture?" I asked with my mouth full.

"Mary Grace!" My mom exclaimed, "Do not eat with food in your mouth! You need to be a lady. And yes, of course I still have that picture. It is in your hope chest in the attic."

I swallowed my food and drank some milk, and asked, "Could you show that picture to me?"

"Well, not this evening, Mary Grace. You need to do your chores and then your homework, and I have to see all of your siblings off to bed." She said.

I drudgingly did my chores. I hated chores, although sometimes I didn't mind them, but this evening, I did not like them. After doing all my chores and finishing up the math problems, I read my book. I then took the Bible near my bed and wrote down the scripture that Nevaeh had shared with me, Hebrews 6:19. I read it again and again, wondering when it would have a different meaning. For now, it soothed my soul, and I felt so much better as my eyes grew heavier. I fell asleep, with the scripture on my mind.

The next morning, I read the scripture one more time, knowing that I would need it. I got up early, at 4:00 a.m., got dressed, and did my morning chores. My mom had made a good breakfast, perhaps knowing that I needed one, after feeling so sad the day before. Usually, I ate cold cereal or cream of wheat, but this morning, we had eggs and bacon. It was a treat to eat such a good meal, as we did not have a lot of money, but my mom let us splurge that morning. My dad was already gone to work when my brothers, sisters, and I sat down for breakfast.

After breakfast, my siblings and I waited for the bus to school. I had three sisters and two brothers. My brothers were identical twins, and were the oldest of my siblings, although Solomon was born first. John was the second born, but he was just as bossy. They were seniors in high school and very athletic. Being an athlete was very difficult for those of us who lived on ranches, but my brothers made it work. The coaches worked with them and one of the coaches, who lived close by, drove them home after practice. My brothers were tall and strong. They were used to bailing hay and branding cattle. Many girls thought they were cute, but they were my brothers, so I didn't see them that way. If they didn't look like John Travolta, they weren't cute. Ruth, my oldest sister, was a sophomore in high school. She was a "book worm," always reading. She wanted to be a teacher in the future and often corrected my spelling. She made me read books that didn't interest me, but I also was an avid reader, so I was glad she recommended the classics. My other older sister, Mary Bella, was a freshman in high school. She was very beautiful; some said she was the "prettiest," although mom often said we were all pretty. She had made the varsity cheerleading team at the beginning of this year. My brothers kept a close eye on her because all the senior boys wanted to date her, and my dad was very strict. She would wait after practice for our brothers, and Coach Gil brought them all home. I was next in line and was extremely awkward. I was in fifth grade, and many teachers said I was the smartest of all my siblings. I had a baby sister, Esther, and she was the cutest of us all. We all had dark brown eyes or hazel eyes, but Esther had blue eyes, a hint of our European ancestry. She loved to play with her dolls, which were actually all of our dolls passed down to her. She had more dolls than the rest of us. She was in first grade and was quite a character. Although we all rode the same bus, Esther liked to sit with her friends, who she often received gifts from. My mom stopped trying to give back the gifts because the parents were aware of the exchanges. I often thought she would be the family politician. She had a way of making promises and people actually believed her. She just had to bat her beautiful blue eyes.

When I entered the bus that morning, I did not see my best friend Sarah. I began worrying about her because she never missed school. Even when she had a cough or wasn't feeling good, she was always on the bus to school. I sat down next to Ruth, who was reading a book and didn't even notice me. I felt fear but remembered what Nevaeh had said about fear. Fear brought about punishment, so I asked Jesus to be my anchor in this ship called life. In my heart, there was hope. In my mind, there was strength. Anxiety went away from me. I reminded myself that I had courage. When you are aware of the pain around you, it can no longer take over your life. Your spirit rises above the sadness. My spirit had been revealed. I feared no evil.

CHAPTER

5

Just as tears calm the soul, rain cleanses the earth.

*Love is the ultimate act of valor that drives
agony away from this world. It never fails.
I know love. Love heals the deepest wounds.
Love is a gesture, a hug, a smile, and the colors of a rainbow. It is the greatest gift in life.*

When we arrived at school that morning, there were police cars in the parking lot. I could not believe, like a scary movie, dread was everywhere, but I had courage. God was with me. I did not have to be frightened. I lifted my head up high as I walked down each step of the school bus. I felt like a Super Hero when I marched into the school building.

"Mary Grace!" I heard someone scream.

I was taken back by someone yelling my name, but I imagined having a cape. Nothing was going to make me fearful. Okay, actually, I was a little bit scared, but I kept reminding myself that I had Super Powers! I could make fear disappear from me and from this school.

I looked in front of me. There was no one. I looked behind me. Nothing or no one was behind me. From the corner of my eye, I could see Sarah running towards me.

"Walk, Sarah!" The duty teacher demanded.

She stopped running, but she paced herself, walking as fast as the duty teacher would allow. I saw tears running down her cheeks.

I walked quickly towards her and put my arms around her little body, which was trembling and asked, "Why all the tears?"

I listened carefully because her words were mumbled from crying. "My grandma was telling my mom last night that Hope was going to live in a foster home. Hope's dad was accidentally shot by Hope's sister. They arrested her sister and sent Hope away from this town. I don't know why they arrested her when it was an accident. We are terrible friends. She was our friend and we weren't there for her."

Suddenly, I didn't feel like a Super Hero. Sarah was right. We *were* terrible friends. We were Hope's only friends, and we let her down. I began crying too when the bell rang. One of the duty teachers walked up to us and knelt down besides us.

"I'm going to walk you two to the counselor's office and I will let Ms. Greene know where I sent you." She said to us.

We held each other side-by-side as we walked to the counselor's office. I had never been to the counselor, but I knew Sarah had because she went to a small group for children who had lost a parent or a loved one.

The duty teacher whispered to the counselor, and the counselor handed us some Kleenex. The counselor kneeled down beside us.

"Can I give you girls a hug?" She asked.

We both nodded yes. Sarah began crying some more, which made me sob. The counselor took some more Kleenex and wiped our faces.

She pulled out two chairs and said, "Why don't you girls sit down and we can talk."

"Sarah, you know who I am, but I don't think you and I have had the pleasure of meeting. Mary Grace, correct?" She asked.

"Yes, I'm Mary Grace Martinez." I said.

It was a small community, so I wasn't surprised she knew my name.

"I'm Dr. Farah." She said.

She gently touched my hand, which was on the table. "I'm glad to meet you, Mary Grace, and am sorry we are meeting under these circumstances."

Sarah looked up and said, "We are so sad because we were terrible friends to Hope. She needed us, and we weren't there for her. Now she's going into a foster home, and she has no mom, and her dad is dead! This hurts so much."

Sarah cried some more while the counselor continued to wipe her face with Kleenex. I looked on the table and noticed four boxes of Kleenex. I began thinking that the counselor must have many students who cry. I looked up at the counselor who was consoling Sarah.

"Did you know Hope's sister accidentally shot her dad? The police arrested her, and we don't understand. It was not on purpose. Everyone makes mistakes." I explained to the counselor.

"Well," the counselor began. "None of this is your fault. You girls are not terrible friends. If you could have predicted this would happen, you would have said something. You can't blame yourselves. None of us could have known this would happen. You didn't let her down."

She hesitated to speak for a moment. "I also want to encourage you not to share this information with anyone because it is a very sensitive issue. This is a lot for Hope and her sister to endure, and many people in the community are coming together to get all the facts and support the family. Please promise me, girls, you won't talk to other students about this unfortunate event, even when all the facts are known. I'm so sorry you girls have been exposed to such sad news. It is hard for everyone."

We promised not to talk about the things we had heard. The counselor then pulled out some paper and crayons.

"Would you girls like to draw a picture?" She asked.

Sarah and I agreed, so we began to draw and color a picture. I drew a picture of Hope. I wanted Hope to be happy, so I used pink and red colors. I drew a sun and colored it yellow and a new house for Hope. I colored the house a light orange.

"Who are these people?" Dr. Farah asked me.

I pointed to the little girl. "This is Hope, and all these people are her new family. And see? She's happy. She has a new home and the sun is out. I'm making a rainbow because it just rained, but the sun came out. There is always a rainbow after it rains. Nevaeh told me that after God cries for his children and gets mad at people who hurt his children, which is why the thunder is loud...well, that's what Nevaeh says...God still shows us he loves us and is there for us when he paints a rainbow in the sky. God even loves us when we hurt each other, so although we hurt Hope by not being there for her, he is going to give her a new family. He is going to show her he loves her after the storm. See, this is the rainbow he will make for her."

I pointed to the beginning of what was going to be the most beautiful rainbow I had ever drawn. Nevaeh told me that some people go through a lot of pain. I had never known anyone who had gone through all this sadness before, but I knew Hope must have felt hurt. I looked at Hope in my picture. I knew she would be okay. She had to be fine.

"That is very profound, Mary Grace." Dr. Farah said to me.

She turned her attention to Sarah. "Tell me about your picture, Sarah."

I looked over at Sarah's drawing. There was a little girl in a dark forest. The little girl has no arms and no feet. She also only had eyes, but no nose or mouth. Sarah had colored the trees black, and there were no leaves or no roots.

I glanced up at Dr. Farah, who seemed concerned, but she asked anyway. "What is your picture about, Sarah?"

Sarah responded. "This is Hope. She is lost in the woods. She has no one. No one loves her. No one was there for her. Everyone let her down."

"I know, Sarah, you think there is no one there for her, but I know first-hand there are people who are there for her. You did not let her down. You are not responsible for things you can't control. The most important thing is that you and Mary Grace love her. I want you to draw another picture, Sarah. This time, you show me how you could help Hope feel better."

She gave Sarah another blank sheet of paper. Sarah looked at my picture as I was finishing the rainbow.

Sarah took out bright colors and drew a big rainbow.

"Did you say God paints rainbows to show us he loves us?" Sarah asked me.

"Yes, that's what Nevaeh always says. Nevaeh said it's a promise to never flood the world again. It's a covenant that God gives us, but Nevaeh says it's more than just a promise. It's a reminder that God is in control even when we get the worst rain storms in our lives." I replied.

Under her rainbow, Sarah drew a happier picture of Hope. This time she added arms and feet. She drew a smiling face and long yellow hair.

"I'm going to put her hair back, away from her face, so she can see the rainbow. I want Hope to know we love her." Sarah said.

Dr. Farah responded. "I know where Hope is staying, and if you girls let me, I would love to share your drawings with her. Would you girls let me give them to her?"

With great big smiles, Sarah and I said yes. We were so excited to know that Hope would get our masterpieces of her. She would know we loved her by the pictures we drew for her. Love would conquer her deepest cuts. Even the darkest forest could not separate Hope from our colorful rainbows. Our friendship would somehow find its way to Hope.

CHAPTER

6

Faith is the essential substance of hope.

You help me find the faith I need in the saddest, most heartbreaking days of my life. Building memories, baking bread, dancing, laughing, and telling stories gives me confidence that material things are temporary but relationships are everlasting.

A few weeks had passed, and I walked over to Nevaeh's house with a pumpkin pie and my "healing box." I put the pie in the box so I wouldn't drop it. In addition to the pie were the handprints of what was going to be a turkey. My mom had given me the painting a few days after she told me about it.

I knocked on the door and could see Nevaeh rushing over to open it.

She embraced me, "Hola, my friend. It is so great to see you!"

I handed her the box and said, "I baked you a pie. You are always baking for me, so I begged my mom to let me make *you* a pie. My dad brought a few pumpkins home from work, and my mom and I made two pies, one for you and one for us."

"So, the pumpkins were about 3 pounds each?" She asked.

"How did you know?" I answered her question with another question.

"I just know, darling! I enjoy baking and know about the weight of pumpkins. I like to think about things like that." She answered, winking at me.

She closed the door behind us, walked over to the table, and placed the box on top of it. She opened the box, and I looked up at her great big smile.

"What a treat, Mary Grace!" She exclaimed. "You are so thoughtful."

I replied, "I learned it from you, Nevaeh. Plus I wanted to cheer you up because last time I saw you, you were so sad."

Nevaeh laid the pie on to a cutting board and covered it with a clean kitchen towel. She picked up the picture in the box.

"What is this?" She asked.

"Well, I just put the pie in the box, but it's like yours, Nevaeh. It's my very own 'healing box.' I made one just like your basket." I proudly said.

Nevaeh covered her mouth and I could see tears in her eyes.

"This is the sweetest thing I have ever heard." She quietly stated.

"I want to be just like you. I want to be able to tell beautiful stories about my loved ones. I want to share my sadness with others, to build my hope." I responded.

Nevaeh reached out for my hand, put the painting back in the box, and we walked into the living room. She put the box on the couch and told me to sit down next to it. She said she would be right back.

A few minutes later, she walked back into the living room with her basket. She sat next to me and placed the basket on the other side of her body.

"Okay, you share first what's in your box, and I will share another memory in my basket." She said.

I opened up my box. I looked at the handprints that evoked many feelings and many memories. I pulled it out of the box.

"When I was in third grade, we made paper turkeys with our handprints for our parents. We used paints and our right hand to represent the feathers. Our teacher gave us a template of the turkey's faces, and we added our handprints for the plumes. We each made one turkey. My best friends, Sarah and Hope, and I had finished our turkeys and we were waiting for them to dry. Since the other students were still working on their turkeys, we decided to make a turkey with all of our handprints and give it to our teacher. We asked if we could have one of the extra templates. Our teacher agreed, and we created a turkey with all of our handprints. It was actually very beautiful and colorful." I said, remembering that wonderful, fun Friday.

I continued, "Then Mark Freed and Peter Romero ruined our turkey by touching it with their hands and putting paint on the face of our turkey. We were so mad, so we began splashing paint on their clothes. Our teacher had us all march to the principal's office after she cleaned us up as much as she could. Now Mark and Peter had been to the principal's office many times, but my friends and I had never been in trouble. On that day, we were all paddled, but I remember when the principal had us waiting in front of his office, we could hear him yelling at Mark and Peter. We kept laughing, Nevaeh. It wasn't really funny, and we were in trouble, but we couldn't stop giggling. When we were paddled, Sarah cried the most, and Hope and I teared up, but as we were waiting for our parents to arrive, we all had to hold back our laughter."

I paused, thinking about that day, "Do you think Hope will be okay? Sarah and I made drawings of rainbows, and the counselor said she would give them to her. We were not the greatest friends, but if we had predicted what Hope and her sister went through, we would have been better friends. We just didn't know."

I felt the tears intensifying up in my eyes. Nevaeh put her arms around my shoulders. She looked at the ruined turkey in my hand.

"That was a lovely story!" She exclaimed. "Hope is blessed to have a friend like you, to remember her. You have memories of people who are still here, and that is a beautiful thing. Just have faith, my little friend that things work out for the best. I wish I could tell you that Hope will be okay, but I can't predict the future. No one can. What I can say is when she gets sad, I bet she will remember the rainbows in your drawings. She might even reminisce about the turkey that the boys ruined. The point is, faith is something we cannot see, but we trust that in spite of everything, when people are hurting, God will send an angel. You and Sarah were angels for Hope when you created the drawings of rainbows. I promise."

Nevaeh wiped my tears, and I put the turkey painting back in my box.

"Now it's your turn." I said.

She looked into her basket, searching. It took her some time but then she pulled something out. Nevaeh took out a handkerchief and held it for a few minutes. I kept looking at her, hoping she would look back at me, but she stared at the handkerchief—the one her mom had in her hand the day her dad left to Normandy. She then told me she carried it to the hospital after she received a phone call from the nurse. When she saw her mom in the emergency room the day she died, she wiped the lipstick off of the lips of her mom, who looked as if she were sleeping. She said she did not know why it bothered her so much that her mom still had lipstick on her mouth. She said her mom would surely not wear lipstick when she slept. As she told me this story, she chuckled, saying to me that we do the most impractical things at a time like that, a time when your life changes after losing the one person who gave you strength. She looked into my eyes and carefully told me that it is at your weakest, most unfounded moments that you find your soul, your purpose, and even yourself.

"I lost my faith when my mom died, but I realized after losing my mom that faith is not easily attained. It only makes things possible. I realized at the most frail times of my life, when things seemed harder than ever, I could eventually rely on faith because I rose above the pain. I became strength. Strength is faith in motion." She explained.

"In the Bible, Jesus was a great example of faith." She continued. "While fishing with his disciples, there was this huge storm. Imagine being in the middle of the Sea and the rain is coming down, the fishing boat is riding the high waves, almost being taken down by the currents, and the fear in the disciples' hearts knowing this could be their last day on earth. Jesus, however, was fast asleep. He might have even been snoring a little bit, and his disciples were angry at him for seemingly having no care in the world. Well, Jesus had faith. He was not focused on the storm but instead he was focused on God, so when the disciples wake him up, Jesus is able to calm the storm. It is his faith that allows him to sleep through the storm. It is his faith that gives him the confidence to calm the storm. It is his faith that knows God is in control, so he can sleep and dream, and yes, even snore!"

At first, we laughed because her story had some humor. I had never thought of Jesus snoring, but it was rather cool to imagine him to be like my dad, a man like any other man. What made him different was his faith, even during the storms.

Together, Nevaeh and I mourned, knowing that our faith had been tested by the loss and sadness of people who were important to us, but we passed the test because we believed in the possibility of everything working out at the end. We knew we were going through the storms in life, but we could have faith to calm them. We had the hope and the courage too. We not only became strengthened by our weakness, we were sure of faith because life had taught us that eventually, somehow, someday, things worked out, perhaps not as we want them to, but as they need to. The God of our universe was in charge, and we have no control of the universe. We only have control of our faith. We could wake up from a deep sleep when life was chaotic because of our faith in God, who would always calm the storms.

CHAPTER

7

God, the Designer of the stars, is my refuge.

There is a time for everything in life. There is a time for change and a time for sameness. There is a time for laughter and a time for sadness. There is a time for friendship and a time for losing friends. There is a time for making memories and a time to only think about what is worth remembering.

I don't know why things seemed to change between Sarah and me. She had been my best friend since before we even started school. We were like two peas in a pod, always together in school, but by the end of fifth grade, things began to be different. Sarah had begun sharing secrets with other girls, more popular girls. She was always more beautiful than me, but my larger frame and glasses never seemed to bother her, not until recently. Every time I would talk to her, she would tell me she had other things to do, but then I would see her with the popular crowd during lunch. I wrote her a letter, but she never responded or even addressed anything that I said. Sarah stopped saving a place for me to sit on the bus, so I sat with my sister, who was always reading. I could see Sarah from a distance, and she seemed happy, always laughing and smiling with her new friends. It hurt me so much.

I spent a weekend with Nevaeh, adding things to my healing box, things that Sarah had given me. I cried because I didn't understand why Sarah no longer wanted to be my friend. She gave me no explanation.

"I have a gift for you," Nevaeh told me as I pulled things out of my box.

She handed me a present, and when I unwrapped it, I was so delighted that it was my very own healing basket.

"Thank you, Nevaeh," I told her. "This means so much to me, especially now that I've lost my best friend Sarah."

The tears began pouring down my face. Nevaeh wiped them with one of her clean towels.

"You haven't lost her, Mary Grace. You are giving her time to come to her senses because she will never find a friend like you. Not ever! Trust me on this one." Nevaeh explained.

I looked up at Nevaeh dramatically crying. I just let the tears come out because I knew Nevaeh understood grief.

"I'm still your friend," she said. "I'll always be your friend, Mary Grace. You will never lose me. I promise."

I believed her because she had always been the one person I could depend on. She was my rock.

I blew my nose in the towel and felt terrible that no one seemed to like me. I realized intellectually that I was an awkward child. In fact, my dad once told me a story about a leafy sea dragon. He loved them because he read many articles about Australia.

My dad, Juan Jose Martinez, always wanted to travel "down under." He collected books and magazines that were about Australia. He said that one day he would visit. I often felt sorry for my dad because he never finished high school and was very smart. He married my mom when he was a senior in high school, and dropped out of high school to work when they became pregnant in the middle of the year. In those days, people got married young, and my grandparents were even younger when they married. My dad was well-educated in the sense that he read a lot of books. My dad loved reading, he enjoyed drinking a six pack of beer just about every weekend, and he was good at woodworking. For many years, he was my hero because he spent his Sundays with his family, taking us to church and having dinner every Sunday night. It was a celebration on Sundays, and he always liked to touch my mom, although we used to tell him to stop. He patted her on the butt and kissed her cheek, telling her she was the most beautiful woman he had ever seen. My mom hated when he drank more than a six pack though because she said he would lose himself and would yell at her. He said some mean things when he was drunk, but I know he said them out of stupidity. It wasn't really him. The alcohol masked my dad's true identity. I remember once he got so drunk that he threatened to shoot himself if my mom left him. I saw him with the gun in his hand as my sisters and I begged him not to do it. It was a scary situation, and when I told Nevaeh about it, my mom grew angry at me, telling me not to tell our family business to anyone. I never did after that, and I learned to deal with the fact that my dad drank to work through the stresses in his life. I prayed for him every day, knowing that one day he would turn to God instead of to alcohol. People have many coping strategies, and alcohol was one of my dads'. The man who drank was the man I dreaded and had a difficult time feeling good about because he was not my dad. He had allowed Satan to get a foothold, but I did not fear evil because God was my anchor, he gave me strength, and I prayed with confidence that in God's timing, my dad would be healed. For now, when he drank, he became someone else, someone I didn't know. He was foreign to me, someone I saw every day but became uncomfortable being around when he wasn't himself. The man who read and dreamed about going to Australia was the man I knew and adored. He was the man God created, and he would be free of the alcohol as long as I believed. He smiled with his eyes, and he looked at my mom like she was beautiful, like Nevaeh's dad looked at her mom. I knew this was who my dad would always be in my heart. God allowed me to see him this way.

He talked about the leafy sea dragon every time I told him I was a loner. He said I was a "spectacular little creature."

He said, "Mi jita, you like to be alone like the leafy sea dragon. You are an independent little girl and will be like this when you're a woman. You will not need a man to take care of you because you are designed to take care of yourself. The sea dragons are protected and they are the official marine emblem for Australia. This is how I see you. You find ways to protect yourself from harm and one day, you will be admired, like an emblem. I know these things."

I believed my dad. He had no reason to lie to me, and I was very independent. I didn't need a boy or my friend Sarah to make me feel special. I was like a leafy sea dragon, mysterious and fragile at times, but strong and independent when I needed to be. One day I would be admired, maybe not by the entire world, but family and friends would look up to me. I just needed to grieve the changes that were happening to me right now. I had to work through all of this, and I would come out a better person. From this point forward, I will not allow Sarah, or anyone, bring me down! It was time to move forward and look upward. I would build other friendships in middle school. I'd meet other leafy sea dragons. I had been liberated!

CHAPTER

8

There is a genuine friend who is closer than a brother.

I have never known more pain than now. I wish agony didn't exist but it is here to stay. One day, there will be no more sorrow or no more tears. One day the tears that we cry will turn to joy. I know this to be true because goodness always comes after bad happens, even if the bad continues for a long time.

I once heard that people remember the beginning of their lives and the end of their lives more vividly than the middle of their lives. The middle is hazier because some things, some moments are made to forget. Middle school, which is in between elementary school and high school, was very difficult for me. It was such a confusing time. It was a painful time. I had few friends I could trust. In fact, it didn't feel like I really had any friends. I often felt alone and lonely.

Nevaeh told me to join a club or sign up for a class that I would enjoy. I signed up for the choir class. I don't know if I sang well but I enjoyed singing with Nevaeh. It was something that we continued to do together after she told me about her dad and that she sang *I'm a Big Girl Now* to the troops. She taught me a beautiful song, *Eres Tu*, which our choir teacher thought sounded great. He let me sing a solo for our Christmas concert when I was in sixth grade. I received a standing ovation, and Nevaeh was cheering loudly, along with all of my family members, who hollered my name. It was a great night!

After the holidays, when we returned to school from the break, I noticed the students being very cruel to our teacher. He was from South Carolina and had an eye problem. His eyes fluttered and although he could see us, his eyes looked as if he were blind. The students were mean to him and often made rude comments about his underarms because he perspired quite a bit, almost abnormally. His name was Mr. Whittaker. He had a white beard and wasn't very tall, but he was extremely talented. He could carry a tune and he taught us Broadway songs.

I remember he even showed us how to sing and dance like Tony Orlando and Dawn. "Hey, has anybody seen my Sweet Gypsy Rose. Here's a picture when she was my Sweet Mary Joe. Now she's got rings on her fingers and bells on her toes. Say, has anybody seen my Sweet Gypsy Rose?" The song began.

It was quite a crowd pleaser. Everyone stood up and clapped after we performed. Mr. Whittaker even went out of his way to get us all tap sticks, made by the high school woodworking class. He also taught a few students how to sing opera songs in different languages.

In my eighth grade year, Mr. Whittaker announced that he would be leaving in December. Of course, some of the most popular kids were the meanest. They planned to give him a going away present, but it wasn't anything nice. It was a can of deodorant. I remember how happy he was to receive a gift from students who did not appreciate him. I mean, he was ecstatic. When he opened the gift, I could see his face turn to a frown, and then he lamented. I thought he was going to cry. It was a terrible joke. I just remember the students laughing. I stayed quiet because I really liked Mr. Whittaker, but I was afraid if I spoke up, I would be shunned by all the students. I felt like such a coward. That day, I stopped by to see Nevaeh and told her what had happened.

"That is so terrible!" She said after listening to how Mr. Whittaker had been treated.

"I should have said something. I should have been brave, but I was so afraid of what the kids would do to me. They already hate me." I said, crying hysterically.

After Nevaeh calmed me down, she went into her bedroom and returned with the healing basket.

"Sometimes, we have no control over things that happen. Sometimes there are other ways to deal with those things." She said. "When Lily began teaching high school, integration was a law that wasn't always being followed. This was a time when black students and white students were segregated and the laws made the public schools put the black and white students in schools together. Many people did not want this to happen and there were parents demonstrating outside the public schools against integration."

She continued. "Lily lived in the heart of Mississippi at this time, and although she still lives there, things are a little better now. However, back then it was difficult to be black. In fact, her husband is black, and although she is Hispanic, the people out there thought she was "light skinned," which is what they called her. She never corrected them because being a light skinned black woman was safer for her than being a Hispanic woman married to a black man."

Nevaeh took out a letter from her healing basket. She looked at me as she opened the letter.

"Dear mom," she started reading the letter. "I hope you are doing well. Corey and I are sometimes so sad when we see the injustices that take place here in Mississippi, and we cannot speak out because we will get beat up, or worse, even killed. Even though Corey is an attorney, his clients are poor and black. His salary is minimal, and mine isn't any better. We fear for our children also because of the way people talk to them, like they are animals or inhuman. I know you keep telling us to move back, but I really feel like I'm making a difference in the student's lives. They are learning how to write well, and we read so many great books. I know they love my classes because of what they write in their essays. I want to share an excerpt from a student's paper. We were discussing segregation, and when some of the students started speaking up about taking things into their own hands, I told them that sometimes we have to wait. We have to wait until the smoke clears the air. We have to wait until emotions are calm. We have to wait until people are willing to listen. We have to wait in silence until the time is right to speak up. A young black girl wrote, 'They tried to silence my voice. What they didn't realize is my children, who while witnessing the injustices that engulfed my very livelihood, were taking notice. What they didn't foresee is they couldn't silence them.' Her father had been accused of raping a white woman and had been lynched. Her family had been through so much and when the white women had her baby, it silenced the entire community. The white woman's baby did not have one ounce of black in her. She falsely accused a black man of rape. Slowly, his daughter is speaking up about it, and one day, she will not be silent and people will take notice. There are many students like her. So, don't you worry about me mom, don't you worry about your grandchildren, and don't you worry about Corey. When the time is right, we will all speak up. We will all stand up. We will no longer be silenced. I love you with all my heart! Keep praying for us. Yours, Lily."

Nevaeh folded the letter, "So, you see, Mary Grace, sometimes we have to remain silent. We can't control people or situations, but we can take the bad and make it into something good. I feared for my daughter, my son-in-law and my grandchildren, but to make it better, I prayed. I encouraged her and lifted her spirit. I did what I could to keep things positive, not perfectly, but as flawless as possible. God is bigger than our problems, and he is bigger than our pain or our fears. We just need to help him a little bit to make some situations better. So, what can you do to make this horrible thing that you witnessed today into something good?'"

"Write Mr. Whittaker a letter or make him a card?" I asked.

"Great idea, and I am thinking that perhaps we can also bake him some cookies." She replied.

In the card, I thanked him for everything he had done and I told him how much I appreciated him. I told him that I would miss him and that he was the best teacher in the world.

When I brought the cookies and the card to Mr. Whittaker the next day, I apologized for all the students.

"You are the greatest teacher I have ever had." I told him.

He did start to cry this time, after he read my note, and then he looked up and smiled at me, "Thank you, Mary Grace. I want you to know that you have a beautiful voice, and you are a talented student. This gesture means a lot to me. I won't forget you."

He reached out to give me a handshake, but I hugged him, turned around and walked out of the choir room. Never in my wildest dreams did I think I would meet my best friend, an unlikely friend.

"Wow, Mary Grace, that was so nice of you," Timmy said.

I was startled because I didn't want anyone to know what I had done. I didn't want the kids to make fun of me.

My face turned red, and he knew I was embarrassed.

"Don't worry, I won't divulge your little secret." Timmy said sarcastically as I tried to walk away from him.

Timmy, or Timoteo, which was his 'real name' was not very popular either. We were both considered weird. He had two older brothers, who played football with my brothers, but Timmy got his name because people said he was supposedly nothing like his brothers. He was fragile and sickly. He had epilepsy and was unable to play football and run track like the athletes in his family. Timmy was a mommy's boy because she was over protective of him. When we were in elementary school, I remember he was teased for wearing diapers. He was incontinent upon having seizures often. I overheard his mom telling my mom that when Timmy was a baby, he had many fevers, and the doctors thought this was the cause of his seizures, but they didn't know for sure. As Timmy grew older, he refused to wear the diapers, and we all knew that because when he had a seizure, he would urinate in his pants. Some of our fellow classmates were so cruel, but he remained positive.

I turned to Timmy as he continued to follow me, "Please don't tell anyone." I pleaded.

"Your little secret is safe with me." He replied.

We just stood there, looking at one another. He was such a good-looking boy. He had grey eyes and long eyelashes. His lips were thick and he had perfectly straight white teeth.

"Mary Grace, you are such a sweetheart." He continued.

"You're not mocking me, are you?" I asked, just to be sure.

He started to chuckle, "Are you kidding me? That was the sweetest thing I've ever seen anyone do to another person that no one likes. I won't tell anyone, even though it is such a kind gesture. I wish I could tell everyone, but you know something?"

"What?" I asked.

"God and all the angels know too, so that's alright by me."

He grabbed my hand and asked me to have lunch with him that afternoon. When we ate together, we just laughed. He had such a great sense of humor. What was even more incredible is that we rode the same bus, so we began sitting together.

Funny how one act of kindness can lead to meeting someone so great that they make what we want to forget worth remembering! I hated mostly everything about middle school, but I loved meeting Timmy. He used to tell me that there are two kinds of people in this world. There are people who teach us how to be and there are people who teach us how not to be. Timmy was kind and generous and funny. He taught me how to be those things. He eased the pain of middle school. I had finally found another leafy sea dragon. He made my tears disappear. He gave me glimpses of what life without pain looked like. He made me realize that no matter what other people thought of him or me, what we cared about was my opinion of him and his opinion of me. We weren't sad anymore because we had discovered what was really important about one another, our kindness and compassion, our tenderness and understanding. There was a lot of bad in our lives because we were teased and no one really liked us, but we took those very things that crushed our spirits, turned them around, and built each other up. We brought each other joy. We made something good out of something bad. We chose love over hate.

CHAPTER

9

Justice, like integrity, is transparency of truth.

*Justice will prevail. Sometimes we live to
see it and other times we know it is coming.
Darkness always comes to light, just like the
sun comes up every morning even after the
darkest night. It's just a matter of time.*

During the summer before high school, we began reading about
Rachel, Hope's sister. Her name was never printed in the papers,
but we all knew who they were writing about. It had been over three
years before her trial was set and she was going to be tried as an adult.
It was difficult to understand why the court system even allowed this
trial to occur. I mean, since then, the entire town had stood behind
Rachel and Hope. Their dad was not a terrible man. He was a poor
man just trying to raise two daughters by himself. I kept reading that
poverty was not a reason to accuse someone of a crime.

I didn't know exactly what was going on, only what was in the
papers, and what we read in the papers focused on the family's lack of
wealth. It seemed like everyone was hooked on Rachel's trial. Rachel
had allegedly dropped the gun while cleaning their small casa, and

a shot was fired, killing her dad immediately. No one could make sense of the fact that she was arrested, but her bail had been paid by the community, and she was living with a foster family. She wasn't allowed to live with Hope, but Hope went to every hearing. Rachel and Hope became the most courageous girls in our community, a symbol of faith and perseverance.

"If people had been more involved in Rachel's life, there wouldn't even be a trial. She doesn't deserve what she is going through." I told Nevaeh.

"You are so right, Mary Grace. Some people did try to help, though. After their mom died, people from church brought over food for several weeks, and they offered to give the girls clothes. Rachel and Hopes' dad was too prideful, or perhaps he didn't want to burden people. I think what you're saying is people shouldn't have given up so easily. Even when people try to make things right, they don't always succeed." She said.

"What do you mean?" I asked. "If people try to make things right, don't they succeed? I think people should have kept coming back, even when they were turned away."

"Yes, but sometimes as human beings, we give up. No matter what happens, I always wonder what God is teaching me in every situation, good or bad. Let me show you something." Nevaeh said.

She went into her bedroom and brought out her healing basket. She pulled out several letters piled onto one another. They were wrapped together with silk ribbon.

"These are letters from the drunk driver who hit and killed my mom." She started. "His name was Tito Calle. His blood alcohol level was 2.5 times the legal limit when he ran that red light. People thought I was crazy when I wrote him letters while he was serving his sentence for the death of my mom, but I had to find closure. I had to forgive him. After I wrote to him, he wrote back to me almost immediately. During his trial, he couldn't even look at me in the courtroom, but he could write to me."

She continued. "In these letters is a person who I could forgive. He was pleasant and witty. He had a sense of humor. I actually got to like him, although I hated him for taking my mom away from me. I guess you can say I learned the difference between loving the sinner and hating their sin. In every letter, he apologized. He said he was knocked out unconscious the day it happened, but when he realized what he did, he had a hard time living with himself. He spoke to me about his family. It was painful for me to know that he had two little boys in grade school. When he was arrested, his wife was pregnant with their third child, a girl, and he would never watch her or his boys grow up. He had a job as a mechanic, which barely made ends meet, and his wife had to move in with her parents so she could go back to work after he went to jail. He said he drank a lot because he felt like such a failure. He had a brother who went to college to become an engineer, and he had a great job and a wonderful family life, but Tito was the worthless one, the one who couldn't afford a family but brought children into this world anyway. This made him feel worse."

"Wow, Nevaeh." I said, "At first, I thought I could never forgive him. I thought he was a hollow man, to take your mom from you, but now I feel sad for him and his family. He had a core. I'm so sorry for missing it."

Nevaeh responded, "No, no. This is why I adore you Mary Grace! You want to protect my feelings and yet you are so compassionate for Tito. You have a good heart, and I guess I do too because Tito and I became friends. I even went before the parole board on his behalf to try and get him an early release, but he stayed in jail for his crime."

"After his parole hearing, a terrible thing happened." She said as I saw the tears falling down her cheeks. "He was working out one day and another prisoner hit him over the head with a blunt object and hurt him very bad. He was rushed to the hospital, and by the time I heard about it and drove to the hospital, he had already passed away. When I arrived, his mom asked me what the hell I was doing there. She told me to leave, that it was my fault that he was not paroled and that if my mom hadn't been driving the day he ran the red light, his life would have been different. I was stunned that she would talk to me that way, but then I remembered what Tito wrote about, how his parents couldn't take responsibility for their actions, so I just walked away. I could never understand the justice in this situation. Everybody lost something or someone. I imagined that Tito would be paroled and that he would turn his life around. I thought that by forgiving him, I could let go of the heavy burden I felt in my heart, the burden of not having my mom. When I went to see Tito at the hospital, I was under the impression that he would say something to me, hug me, thank me, or help me bring closure. Instead, his mom blamed him for everything hurtful that had happened to Tito. She needed to do that to feel better, but every expectation had become a living nightmare. We never know the outcome. There is the expectation of life and the reality of life, so now, I expect very little from others. Nothing surprises me anymore, but at least I can go on to remember Tito, not the drunk driver, but the man who had a family, a wife and children who he loved. I wrote to his wife and told her that I was sorry for her loss, that I had let go of the past, and that I knew how much she and their children meant to him. I never heard back from her, and I'm okay with that. I do think about Tito every once in a while, and I know while he was in jail, he read his Bible every day. He sang hymns. He prayed for his children and his wife. He even told me he had been baptized. I am comforted knowing he is in heaven. I believe he is in heaven. Maybe we need tragedies in our lives to bring us closer to God?"

As I grew older, I appreciated the way Nevaeh put things in perspective for me. I could watch Rachel's trial in the papers without any expectations and without any surprises. I cut out every story about Rachel's trial and placed it in my healing basket. It was a way to stay connected to Hope. It wasn't long before we learned that Rachel had been acquitted of all charges. The papers read that she would be reunited with her younger sister and they would be financially supported by an anonymous donor. This was all good and well, but I couldn't imagine the emotional scars that Hope and Rachel faced. However, I imagined Hope looking at the drawings that Sarah and I had sent her in fifth grade and that she had finally witnessed a rainbow, three years after the storm had hit her. Of course, this was not an expectation, just a nice thought. Perhaps God had put it in my head. It was comforting. Besides, I thought, this may have brought Rachel and Hope closer to God. Another nice thought.

The summer before my 9th grade year was very confusing. I had started my period, a late bloomer, and my body had changed a lot. I was still heavy set but I had slimmed down and was beginning to like my body a little more.

Timmy and I spent a lot of time together that summer. He told me to stop calling him Timmy. When I would see him around other people, he would act differently, but with me, he was himself. He tried so hard to be more serious around other people, and he presented himself as a strong, tough guy, like his brothers. However, when he was with me, he was so humble and soft hearted. He talked about reading the scriptures and his relationship with God, which he teasingly stated was the only relationship he would ever have, until I came into his life. He felt God had blessed him with a best friend on earth, and I was truly his friend.

"I'm so tired of people calling me Timmy." He complained one day. "Maybe I am being sensitive, but I am growing out of that name. My parents did name me Timoteo, not Timmy."

"Well, should I call you Timoteo then?" I asked.

"No, now that we're in high school, you can just call me Tim." He said as we started laughing simultaneously.

Every once in a while, Tim made a bigger deal out of something, like outgrowing his elementary school name, but we always found a solution quickly. Nevaeh said we acted like a brother and sister, but I felt closer to Tim than I did with my biological brothers. I mean, Tim and I weren't interested in one another like many thought. We were just close because God had brought us together. God was the one who kept our relationship growing. People didn't believe that two people of the opposite sex could have a relationship like ours. I knew in my heart, however, that a divine intervention is the cornerstone of any great relationship, which is what made it almost perfect.

"I've been studying scriptures about justice, Mary Grace, and God says to let it be his to avenge." He mentioned.

"You do realize there is no justice for us, at least not *worldly* justice." He continued as he picked up the paper about Rachel's acquittal.

"What do you mean, Tim?" I asked.

"Well, no one likes us, right?" He waited for my answer.

"Most people don't like us, Tim." I answered, "Nevaeh likes us and most of our teachers like us, so I have to disagree when you say no one likes us."

"I'm talking about our classmates. What I mean is no one in our grade likes us. They don't like us for no reason. They don't like you because you are too smart for your own good. It is possible they can't relate to your high intelligence. And they don't like me because maybe they're afraid my seizures are contagious. No one wants to live like me, it seems."

"Tim, we shouldn't have any expectations of our classmates. They are missing out. When you and I are together, we have so much fun! They don't get to enjoy your wit and your sense of humor. They aren't privy to all my academic secrets, which, by the way, has helped you enormously. I personally think there is no justice for ignorant people. People who don't like us look at the outside and not at our hearts, which is what matters to God!"

"I just think they are not thinking about the big picture, so I thank God for *his* justice." He said. "God has the big picture already figured out. I believe that our lives are like an empty canvas, and what we put on it is up to us. God gives us opportunities to make things right, to repent of our shortcomings and our sins, but some people don't take the opportunity to do this. Their canvasses are darkness, and God puts colors in our lives, so we see light. I really don't think God judges us while we are on this earth. He wants everyone to inherit his Kingdom. He wants all of us to be saved, so he gives us every opportunity to change and become more and more like his son, the standard, but we aren't perfect, so we have to see God's justice as an opportunity to be holy."

"What colors does he put in our lives?"

"Well," Tim thought for a while, "the color of red could be anger. People are angry for so many reasons, and anger doesn't mean we sin. Anger is a feeling even Jesus felt. It's an opportunity to see red on our canvas and to deal with our anger in a productive way. Blue is sadness, and we are sad when we lose friends or family members. Yellow is a color of fear. People fear what they don't understand. They fear us, for example, because they don't take the time to know us, but we give them the opportunity to see yellow on their canvasses. Red, orange, yellow, green, blue, violet. These colors represent our feelings and the Bible says our feelings can deceive us. Together, however, they create this phenomenon called light. If we discern all of our feelings and why we feel the way we do, then our dark canvas becomes light. All the pain, all the disappointments, all the sadness, all the fears in our lives point us in the direction of holiness because God's justice is light. We walk in the light, Mary Grace, and to some people we are an aroma of life to those who believe in the power of God, but to other people we smell like death because our beliefs make them feel uncomfortable, for reasons they can't even explain."

I enjoyed Tim's company and the way he thought. He wanted to become a minister one day, and he studied the Bible often. He said he read the book of Acts often because it was the beginning of the first century church. He had learned about the Berean Jews, who were of noble character. They heard about God in the synagogues, and they studied the scriptures to build their understanding and their convictions. People needed their own convictions, according to Tim, and only God has the power, in his Bible, to give us those principles, including living in the light and finding justice...God's justice.

We had in fact discovered justice that day. Justice had prevailed because we had been "acquitted" of how others saw us. We accepted one another for who we were, and we were like the colors of the light. We didn't have to pretend or blame one another for our shortcomings. We were free from other people's opinions of us. We had realized God's holiness. We were the aroma of life to those who followed God and to one another, and we were like shining stars following the standard of our brother, Jesus Christ, also known by me as JC. We were blessed. Justice had prevailed. Perhaps, I thought, we could be like the Berean Jews, of great character!

CHAPTER

10

Let nothing or no one dim the light within our souls.

Searching for our place in this world occurs at this time. Looking around and coming to the realization that life as we know it no longer exists. We see the bigger picture, the details of the picture, the colors, and the darkness of life. Sometimes we have to leave things behind in order to move forward.

High school for everyone is a chance to rise above all of our insecurities that middle school seemed to create. For some, high school is a beginning of greater things but then ends up worse than when we started. For others, high school is a stomping ground, a place people get stuck because they never succeed at doing anything else. For me, high school was a chance to learn some skills and leave my community all together.

"Hey beautiful friend!" Tim exclaimed as I climbed up the stairs of the bus wearing high heel shoes. My mom told me I would live to regret it, but it was my first day of high school, and I had to make a good impression. I had my hair up in a bun and had curled the hairs that would not stay in the bun. I had finally gotten new eye glasses and thought I looked really cool because if Elton John could look cool in pink glasses, I could look cool too! I wore a tight fitted shirt, showing off my curves, along with an A-line skirt and a light blazer that my mom insisted I wear, probably to cover up my curvy body. I thought I looked great, but I would soon learn that not everyone else did.

"Hello Tim," I said waiting for him to move his book bag off the seat he had saved for me.

He too was dressed up, wearing a shirt and tie. He wore Levis and cowboy boots. Tim was such a handsome guy, like his brothers, but they came across as stuck up. Tim was down to earth. Our older siblings had already graduated high school, so we had talked about this being our time to shine, to be the light, which was our saying throughout high school.

I could see Sarah in the back of the bus, whispering and laughing. Tim told me not to take it personally, but it was so hard sometimes. She was very popular and had many friends. She had made the Varsity dance team. Tim told me that she would sometimes hang out with his brothers. He said he saw them all smoking pot together, and even though she thought she was better than me, she was heading down a road that would only lead to loneliness. I didn't believe him because from the outside looking in, she had the ideal life.

Tim hugged me as I sat down. He was the best hugger I had ever known and was always complimentary to me.

"You're my best friend!" He said. "I am so excited to have most of my classes with you. I'm going to get straight A's because of you!"

We had done everything to be in the same classes. The only difference was P.E. and gifted. P.E. was segregated, boys and girls, so we could not take that class together. I had a gifted class, and although I begged my mom to keep me out of that class because everyone was so competitive, she refused. It's the law that you stay in the gifted class is all she would say to me. Other than that, we had all the same classes. We were determined to get straight A's and our goal was to graduate top of our class. We were going to do it together. We had planned to go to all the dances together and to travel together after high school.

We wanted to go to Australia because I had told Tim about the leafy sea dragon. We were so excited about our first day of high school.

When we arrived at school, our first class was math. I was so glad Tim got into accelerated Algebra, and I promised I would help him. Only the best students were in this class, so I was relieved that Sarah would not be in our class. She struggled in school, so I knew we would not have any classes together. I just didn't want to be bullied by her and her friends. I don't know what I ever did to be treated this way, but it mattered less and less as time moved on. I had written her many letters and placed them in my healing basket, just as Nevaeh has suggested. It did help because I was able to get out my feelings and tell her how she hurt me. I was able to tell her the meanest things and then let them go. Some of the letters I burned in Nevaeh's wood stove because they were too mean to keep, but I let the things that hurt go. I wouldn't be held captive by my thoughts. Besides, if we had remained friends, I might never have met Tim, and he was great! I mean, I had a best friend and a brother in one package. I was so lucky. No, I was blessed.

Our math teacher was a younger man. He was tall and had blue eyes. He had gone to Harvard and had a degree in engineering. He married a woman from our hometown, so since there were no engineering jobs in this town, he became a teacher. His wife was related to Tim somehow. They were distant relatives. Tim had many relatives who did very well and had college degrees. This was not the norm in our town because most people were blue collar workers, laborers. Tim slipped me a note that said we had it made in this class. Mr. Truman, our math teacher, noticed him passing the note but did not say anything. I think Tim was right. We had it made in this class.

After math class, we went to Biology. It was a larger class, and the teacher, Ms. Lopez, was very scary. She looked like the doll, Mrs. Beasley, was very thin and tall, and she was older than most of the other teachers. She had a reputation for being sarcastic and didn't put up with nonsense. She ran a tight shift, but the students did so well in her class. They learned a lot, and she brought in parts of a cow to dissect every year. Her classroom was very clean and disinfected. She made the students keep it clean. Tim and I would not be passing notes in her class!

We next went to English class. Mrs. Romero was very structured and didn't like excuses, as she kept saying that several times when introducing her class. We would be reading in class and outside of class. Some books we would really enjoy and others we would dislike, she explained to us, but we would read them all.

Our next class was different. Tim went to drafting and I had my gifted class. He gave me a hug and we parted ways. It was at this time when I ran into Sarah and her friends.

"Look at her!" Sarah exclaimed. "She must be trying to look like Miss Piggly Wiggly."

Everyone she was with burst out laughing. They were all looking at me. I held back the tears and moved quickly away from them, but it hurt me so deep. I walked into my class and looked outside the window so no one would notice that there were tears in my eyes. Words cut like a knife. I remembered their canvasses. They would eventually be exposed by the light.

"Good morning class. My name is Ms. Lujan. I am your gifted teacher." She said, after the bell rang, leaning on her desk with papers in her hand.

She was very young and looked like she herself was still in high school. She was a very small lady and had an angelic look. This was her first year as a teacher.

"I know I'm young, but just remember, this class is right before lunch. If you want to get released for lunch on time, you will complete your assignments on time." She explained.

She shared her curriculum with us, and I was very excited about this class. Her class seemed very interesting when she explained all the things we would be doing. I wasn't going to enjoy getting to her class with Sarah and her friends close by, but once I got here, I would be okay.

At lunch, I hurried to the lunch room to meet up with Tim. When I told him what Sarah and her friends had said, he reminded me of how to deal with it, things that Nevaeh had taught us.

"I get teased sometimes about my seizures. In fact, people ask me if I still wear diapers and laugh, which is so cruel. I can't help it, and today people have been making fun of my tie, but in my mind, I talk to God and surrender the problems to him. I bet Jesus would have worn a tie his first day of high school." He said, smiling. "So, like Nevaeh tells us we have to do is to erase the negative out of our minds. You're not Miss Piggly Wiggly and I do not need diapers. My tie is cool."

"Let's put in a new tape." I started as we simultaneously pretended to take out the old tape and put in a new one in our heads. "You are the most awesome friend in the entire world. You have style Mr. Tim because your tie is so debonair, and you are so handsome. You are witty and make me laugh. You give the best hugs and every time I think about you, I thank God."

"And, you are the best friend a guy could ever have. You are beautiful and know all your math facts. You have told me great stories about Australia and when we are together we just laugh. You are an angel to me and I love being with you. You are the kindest person I have ever met, and you are a Godsend, a young woman of noble character."

After lunch, we went to our last three classes, P.E., history and Choir. We had different P.E. teachers, and our classes would be structured. Our history teacher, Mr. McInroy, had a reputation for helping students remember historical events. His class was very interesting, according to my siblings. He was very well respected and had traveled the world, which he brought into the classroom.

Finally, Mr. T, our Choir teacher, whose last name was too difficult to pronounce, was a great musician. He played five or six different instruments and although I didn't think he sang very well, he was in a Blues Band for 20 years before becoming a music teacher and played guitar quite well.

Tim and I were happy with our freshman classes. We were looking forward to spending the next four years together, and although we had plans to travel all over the world after high school, we were just going to take it one day at a time. We were going to savor the moments. We had found our places in high school. Our friendship was all we needed to get through these years and once they were over, we could move on with the rest of our lives. We never had to go back. We just needed to keep moving forward with our new tapes. The old ones had been erased.

11

The prayers of the righteous are powerful.

When life give you lemons, you make lemonade.
When you have no control over life, you pray. Only
God can give us the serenity to accept the things
we cannot change, the courage to change the things
we can, and the wisdom to know the difference.

High school began quickly and moved along even quicker. When we entered our junior year, Tim and I were looking forward to going to all the dances in high school. We still had so much fun together, and our parents allowed us to stay at Nevaeh's overnight sometimes. We loved hearing her stories from treasures she pulled out of her basket. We were surprised to learn that she once had an alcohol problem.

"I started drinking after my mom died." She told us as she held the Twelve Step Book. "I drank because life was too painful to deal with sober."

She continued, "I was an angry drunk. You know, that is why I have few true friends in this town. Some people never forgave me for my hateful words, and I don't blame them. I can't even remember how many years I drank or all the mean things I said because some of those days I blacked out for weeks. I've been sober for most of my life, but in those few years that I drank, I said so many horrible things to people. I realized that sometimes, we can only forgive ourselves. In the twelve step program, we admit that we are powerless over our addiction. We have to make a list of all the people we have offended, and then we have to try to set things straight. I worked hard on my sobriety, and I went out to many people I had wronged and tried to reconcile with them. Some of them threw me out of their businesses and even their homes. Not everyone forgives us, you know, so sometimes all we can do is seek God's mercy and then we must forgive ourselves."

Nevaeh was open about her past. She had accepted it, and she knew that drinking wasn't the best way to deal with stress or disappointment or grief. She told us she did not have any self-control over alcohol, so when she became sober, she couldn't drink at all.

"Some people have to stay away from drinking alcohol because they use it to destroy themselves." She warned. "I am tempted to drink again because it takes away my pain, but I choose to stay sober. There are healthier ways to deal with our lives, and alcohol is not one of them."

Tim and I were getting ready to go to our junior dance together, and we knew we would not drink. We didn't want to deal with life using destructive habits. We had made arrangements to stay with Nevaeh overnight, and we got ready at her house.

Nevaeh combed my hair and helped me with my dress. I wore a dress that she had made for me. It was all white and I looked like a bride. When I saw Tim, I smiled. He looked so handsome in his blue suit and tie, and I knew we would have fun together, no matter what people thought of us.

When we went to the dance, people were actually very nice to us. They thought we were a cute "couple," but we were just best friends. We wanted to keep our brother and sister relationship as the focus, not anything else, because it was great. Tim pointed out that the scriptures did say we, our relationship, should not have even a hint of sexual immorality, so we kept our relationship pure.

"You are my sister in Christ and my only friend. You do know what this means?" He asked.

"What does this mean?" I asked a question with a question.

"I'm probably going to die a virgin!"

"Me too!" I exclaimed.

We looked at one another and burst out laughing. After the dance and as we drove to Nevaeh's house, Tim began to have a seizure. It was like no one I had ever seen. It was later described as a grand mal seizure, and it scared me. I heard him screaming and although it lasted for just a few minutes, it seemed like a long time. Tim was unconscious and when he came to, he said he had a very bad headache and wanted to sleep. I kept repeating his name, and although he seemed to look at me to acknowledge he had heard me, I wasn't sure if he was okay. I drove fast and arrived at Nevaeh's house frantic. She must have been waiting up for us because she waved at us as we drove up to her house. With the truck still running, I ran to the passenger side. Nevaeh saw my desperate facial expression, and so she rushed over to us.

I shouted, "Tim just had a terrible seizure! He is not responding to me, Nevaeh!"

"Be calm. How long did it last?" she asked.

"Just a few minutes, I think, but then he was out and when he woke up, he said he had a terrible headache and just wanted to sleep!"

As I was talking, she put her hand on Tim's forehead. "Are you sure it didn't last more than five minutes?"

"I'm sure."

"Did he have another one?"

"No."

Just then, Tim opened his eyes. "I'm okay. I can hear everything you're saying. I haven't had a grand mal seizure like this in a long time, but I will be okay. I'm just really tired."

"I talked to your mom, Tim, and she told me what to do if you ever had a grand mal seizure. She said it would pass. Can you get out of the truck?" Nevaeh asked.

As she helped him get out of the truck, I turned it off, and closed the driver's door first, and then the passenger door after Tim had exited it. I noticed he had been incontinent, but he was among friends, so it didn't matter.

"I want to go to the bathroom, but I will be okay." Tim said as we entered Nevaeh's house.

Nevaeh gave us a big hug once she knew we were inside, safe, saying, "Group hug! I love you guys. I am so blessed to call you young people my friends. I stopped feeling lonely because of you two."

Tim slowly walked to the bathroom, and even though we offered to help him, he refused. He leaned on the walls until he entered the bathroom.

After a few minutes, Tim, sounding like himself, asked me to bring him his overnight bag. I could hear the water running and closed my eyes when he cracked the door open to retrieve it.

I changed into my pajamas and put on a robe. Nevaeh took his soiled clothes to soak them, and she put his suit pants in a plastic bag for dry cleaning.

Tim came out wearing a robe too. We looked at each other and began laughing. We were just like siblings it was so funny. We sat on the couch, and watched Nevaeh as she pulled what looked like a letter from her healing basket.

Nevaeh cleared her voice and started reading, "Dear Nevaeh, I know you are going through a lot right now, so I want to encourage you to pray. Jesus prayed all the time, especially as he travelled to lonely places. You are in a desolate place in your life right now and having a relationship with God is like having a best friend. What would happen if you stopped talking to your best friend or your best friend stopped talking to you? We communicate with God when we pray, and he talks to us when we read our Bibles. After hearing Jesus pray, his disciples begged Jesus to teach them to pray. First of all, Jesus had a relationship with his dad. He even called him what is our equivalent to "daddy." Second, the Our Father was to teach his disciples to pray. We pray this every time we attend our A.A. meetings, but the prayer has a much deeper intent. So, here goes as I try to show you how Jesus taught his disciples to pray:

- Our Father is the introduction, as if we were to go to our dad and greet him with awe.

- Who art in heaven means wherever we go, he is right beside us and one day we will be together for eternity.
- Hallowed be thy name is thinking about God's name--the Great I Am, the holy one, the one we aspire to imitate. Look around and you will see all of God's creations, in the trees and the streams; in the birds and the tiniest insects; as his sun rises and his sun sets. God is everywhere.
- Thy Kingdom come means that his kingdom is within us and we must always be joyful as if the kingdom is here. He made it practical for us to be a part of his Kingdom when he came to us as a man.
- Thy will be done on earth as it is in heaven, reminding us that no matter what happens, God is in control and we must strive to do his will, to love, to share our faith, and to be understanding. We need to notice that he is working things out on earth to prepare us for heaven.
- Give us this day our daily bread means God will meet our needs, one day at a time. We are more important than the birds and the flowers, and he wants us to know he will take care of us. We must believe this, and we must ask.
- And forgive us our trespasses as we forgive those who trespass against us, so we must forgive as we receive forgiveness.
- And lead us not into temptation means God will not allow us to be overwhelmed by temptation. He will always find us a way out.
- But deliver us from evil, and God will deliver us from sin.

So when you pray, think of God in this way, just as Jesus did. Let your prayers be powerful and effective! Prayerfully, your sponsor Monique."

Nevaeh continued, "Join me in prayer."

Tim and I smiled at one another and then at Nevaeh, and we communicated with our dad that evening and many evenings to come. God was our daddy, and we must always talk to him in prayer. This would be the most awesome relationship we would ever have in all of our lives.

The next morning Nevaeh made us breakfast and sent us home after we ate. I wanted to stay and help her wash the dishes, but she knew my dad needed his truck. As Tim and I drove down the dirt roads of our little community, he sang to me, a song by the Bee Gees, "Nobody gets too much heaven no more. It's much harder to come by. I'm waiting in line."

I joined in and we sang the rest together, "Nobody gets too much love anymore. It's as high as a mountain and harder to climb. Oh you and me girl got a lot of love in store. And it flows through you. And it flows through me. And I love you so much more. Then my life, I can see beyond forever. Everything we are will never die. Loving's such a beautiful thing. On you make my world, a summer day. Are you just a dream to fade away..."

As we sang the chorus again, I had already driven up to his house, and we continued to sing until he collected his belongings and closed the passenger door.

I sang the rest of the song as I continued driving down the road. I decided to pray and talk to God in the way Jesus had taught his disciples to pray, so I turned down the music.

"Daddy. I like the sound of that, daddy, and I love you so much. When I think of your power I know heaven is so close to me. I can see heaven around me, in the sky and the clouds. Heaven is a smile from a friend and the different colors of a rainbow that make us light. You are the most holy man in this world, and I thank you for putting people in my life who show me glimpses of you, like Nevaeh and Tim, my dad and mom and all my siblings. I see your sky and think of your beauty. I look at your mountains and think of your strength. I see the birds in the air and know you meet their every need. Yet, I am so much more important to you than they are, and you will meet my needs too. I look to the trees and think of the deep roots you have given me. No storm can harm me because you are always with me. Help me, dad, to always shine and be a reflection of what heaven might look like. Let me express your kingdom within me, in my thoughts and in my words and especially in my actions. Please help me to accept your will, even when I don't understand why so many sad things have happened to Nevaeh or why Tim has seizures or I don't understand why my dad drinks, and God, I don't know why Rachel and Hope have had to suffer, but in my lifetime, please let me see your purpose and your will in all of this because everything that happens points us to heaven. Help me to take one day at a time, to see your blessings in every moment and even in every tear. Forgive me for my mean thoughts about others, especially my friend, Sarah and I pray that she forgives me too. Please, daddy, absolve me for my shortcomings, for when I slam doors and for when I deal with my anger in a temperamental way. Help me to walk away from sin and to walk in the path of righteousness, being kind and gentle and compassionate, just like your son and my brother Jesus. Keep my family and my friends safe, father, and thank you for music that reminds us of heaven and of you. I love you so much, daddy, and it is in your son's name I pray. Amen."

It felt so good to pray. I was so excited to build a relationship with God, who I could talk to every day, just like a real person. I could feel him all around me, so I turned up the music again, replaying the song, but this time I sang the lyrics to God, my daddy, the Great I Am!

CHAPTER

12

Forget what is behind and move forward.

Letting go and letting God is easier said than done. Focusing on the here and now is what must be done in order to surrender it to God. Then we can come to terms with what has been done, the things that have offended us and the things we have done to offend others.

During the summer before our senior year, there seemed to be so many parties, none of which Tim nor I were ever invited to. We didn't mind though. We would have our own prayer parties, walking down to the little stream on Nevaeh's property to find a quiet place to pray. We sat on a large rock near the stream on Nevaeh's property and talked to God. People might think we had lost our mind if they heard us talking to God, but we didn't care. Some nights we would sing hymns and dance as we sang. We could feel God's presence. He was with us.

After praying, we would walk back to Nevaeh's house and spend the night. Some nights we would stay up all night in her living room reading the Bible and talking about the word of God. Then we would doze off on the couches. Nevaeh would wake us up in the mornings, and she would always make breakfast for us.

At the end of July, one dreary night, Nevaeh received a very disturbing call from Sarah. Nevaeh was having a difficult time understanding her, so Nevaeh gave me the keys to her truck and told me to go pick her up. She was at a party down the road, and we could see the smoke from the bonfire. Sarah had walked to a nearby house and called Nevaeh. We weren't sure which house, but Tim and I would find her.

Earlier that day, we had been baking bread and muffins at Nevaeh's house. Tim was feeling down because he was having several seizures that year.

"The doctors told my mom that the seizures would stop as I grew older, but I keep having them. I feel God made a mistake with me. People say it's a seizure disorder, and a disability. They make me sound like a leper. I'm beginning to think God isn't perfect in all his creations." He told us as we kneaded the bread together.

Nevaeh wiped her hands and went to her room. When she came back to the kitchen, she had a picture a little boy, which was in her healing basket. He was a beautiful child and was smiling big in the picture. His smile was so big, in fact, that I could see his gums, but it was obvious he was happy. I mean, having Nevaeh for a mom would make anyone happy.

"This is my baby boy, Estevan," she said. "He was born with congenital heart disease. My husband left me soon after the medical bills started piling up. I spent almost every penny from the life insurance policy my mom had left me, but I didn't care because I wanted Estevan to live a long life. His heart condition shortened his life, and he died in my arms when he was four years old. Losing a child is the hardest thing I've ever been through. Once I lost Estevan, every other problem seemed easier. At his funeral, I couldn't even speak, but my daughter, who was still a child herself, talked to Pastor Salas about finding a scripture she could read."

Nevaeh turned the picture over, and taped to the picture was a note that her daughter had written to Estevan.

"Dear Estevan," Nevaeh explained that her daughter read this at his funeral. "I don't understand why God took you back. You were so young. I am so sad I only had you for four short years. In those years, you made me happy. Together, we saw the sun in the morning and the stars at night. We laughed until we cried. Even when you were in pain, you smiled at me, to remind me you were still my kind and sweet little brother. I found a scripture that reminds me of you. Psalm 139:14 reads, 'I will praise thee; for I am fearfully and wonderfully made: marvelous are thy works; and that my soul knoweth...' Today, little brother, I praise God because of how he made you, set apart from anyone else, and so we give you back to him today, in the same way that he gave you to us, fearful and wonderful. You made my life better. I'm going to miss you, but you will always be my little angel. Hugs, little brother. I love you...until we meet again, Lily."

We were all crying by the time Nevaeh had read her daughter's name. We stepped away from the dough so tears would not fall into it, but the letter impacted us that day.

"You see, Tim, you came to me and remind me of my angel because you too are fearfully and wonderfully made. You make my life complete. God put you here for a reason and a purpose. One of those reasons was to help me through some of my hardest days when I miss Estevan. I thank God when I think of you." She said to Tim and then turned to me, "And I thank God when I think of you too, Mary Grace."

We dried our tears and washed our hands. We continued to knead the dough.

"You know, it took God six days to create the world." Nevaeh began another conversation.

"I thought it took seven." Tim interrupted.

"He rested on the seventh day." I reminded him.

"Yes, he did rest on the seventh day, but it took six days to create everything on this earth. Imagine all of the birds in the air, the Rainforests, the trees, the mountains, the stars, the animals, the rivers and streams, the oceans, and all the plants and flowers throughout the world. He made all kinds of rocks and water to drink. God made all the planets and the solar system. It took him six days. Yet, it takes him nine months to make us. He weaves us in our mother's wombs. I mean imagine what he must be thinking as he is weaving us. Even I would think about my children before they were born, what they would look like, what they would do in the future, and what they would become. I don't have any idea how many hairs they have on their head, and I couldn't even guess correctly, but God knows how many hairs we have on our head at any given day. He cares what we feel and what we think. He hears our prayers and listens to us when we are in despair. He must watch us sleep and visit us in our dreams, our good dreams. Have you ever seen a baby smile when they are sleeping?" She asked.

Tim and I nodded yes.

"Well, I just know God is visiting them in their dreams. We are like this dough. Sometimes we might put a little more salt or too much water in it. Maybe we add too much flour, so we have to add more water. When we bake the bread, we might not take it out of the oven at the perfect time so it is browner on the top. Sometimes you run out of dough to make the last loaf of bread as big as the others but it is still just as good or just as soft in the middle. I take pride in my baking. Can you imagine how God sees us, his creations, after he finishes knitting us? He makes sure every little hair on our head is accounted for and he gives us the best hugs in our dreams, even better than yours Tim. He doesn't make mistakes. It is people who make mistakes, how they see one another or judge one another. We are the flawed ones when we say negative things about each other, not God."

The bread came out perfect that day, and we noticed our finished products tasted so good. For some reason, the bread tasted better than ever. We were content that day. Things became scary, however, when Sarah made the phone call to Nevaeh later on that evening.

Tim and I got into Nevaeh's truck and went looking for Sarah. It took us several hours to find her, but when we did, she was passed out. We tried to wake her up, but she would open her eyes and say some things we couldn't understand and fall back asleep. Tim and I carried her into the truck and rushed her to the hospital. I was driving very fast because the nearest hospital was 30 miles away. Halfway to the hospital, a police officer stopped us because we were speeding.

Tim was very upset and pleaded with the officer. "Please officer, let us go. Our friend Sarah is very sick."

He used his flashlight to look into the truck. He could see that she would open her eye and her eyeballs were rolling to the back of her head.

"Were you drinking?" He asked me.

"No, and we are not sure what our friend was doing, but she doesn't seem right." I answered his question.

"Why didn't you call the ambulance?" He was on his radio as I was answering him. "Follow me. An ambulance is on its way and will meet us halfway."

The police officer turned on his lights as we followed him. We were almost to the hospital, since we had been driving fast. We only drove less than 10 more minutes when we saw an ambulance on the right side of the road. The police officer pulled over, and the Emergency Medical Technicians, EMT's, were already outside the ambulance waiting for Sarah.

Before they took her out of the truck, they placed a brace around her neck. They tried talking to her but she wasn't responding. Tim was answering questions the police officer was asking him while I stayed with Sarah. The EMT's asked about her allergies and I could not remember if she had any. They also inquired about what she had been taking, but I had no idea. I told them she was at a bonfire and had called us from a neighbor's home. I explained we were not even at the bonfire and had to track Sarah down. I gave them her grandmother's address because she and her mom still lived with her grandmother. The EMT's were able to stabilize Sarah and so they rushed her to the hospital.

The police officer escorted us to the hospital, and we followed the ambulance from a distance behind. When we got to the emergency room at the hospital, the nurses would not let us follow Sarah into the hospital rooms. We had to stay in the waiting room. I called Nevaeh to let her know what was going on, and she had already called my parents, who were on their way to the hospital, and Tim's parents, who told Nevaeh to keep them posted. They did not want to drive all the way to the hospital because they felt they would only get in the way, but they wanted to know when Tim and I got back to Nevaeh's house. I tried calling Sarah's mom, but no one answered, so I thought her mom and grandmother must also be on their way to the hospital.

When my parents arrived, I saw Sarah's mom walking in with my mom. They were both holding Sarah's grandmother's arms, as she was fragile.

"Sientate aqui, mama," Sarah's mom told the grandmother to sit down.

"Donde esta Sarah? Se encuentra ella bien?" Sarah's grandmother asked the nurse standing next to us where Sarah was and if she was okay.

Sarah's mom answered her by telling her she would find out how Sarah was doing and would let her know, "Mamá, déjame ver cómo está Sarah y te lo haré saber."

"Hola abuela Francesca. Tim y yo estamos aquí contigo. No te preocupes." I said, letting Sarah's grandmother know that Tim and I would stay close to her and for her not to worry.

She grabbed my hand and told me in Spanish that Sarah had been doing drugs for two years now. She had been so worried because of the friends she was hanging out with.

Tim and I hadn't seen any warning signs of drug addiction. Sarah had been on the Varsity dance team since our freshman year, and we did notice she hadn't been performing. She always wore her uniform during performances. Lately she sat next to the coach, so we just assumed she hadn't made grades, but we didn't know she had been doing drugs. Maybe the drugs were affecting her grades. We didn't know the details.

We stayed at the hospital all night, and I kept dozing off. At about 6:00 a.m. Sarah's mom woke me up. Sarah was asking for me. I looked to the left and Tim had fallen asleep and was leaning on my mom's shoulder. I stood up and followed Sarah's mom into a darkened hospital room. Sarah was hooked up to a machine that was monitoring her heartbeat and her blood pressure. She had an I-V that was administering fluids inside her vein on her arm.

"Mom, could I please talk to Mary Grace alone?" Sarah asked.

"Of course, mija." Her mom responded and walked out the door.

"I don't have any right to ask this of you, but please come close to me, Mary Grace, like when we were little girls. Hold me tightly." She begged.

I crawled close to her and put my arms around her. I don't understand why so many tears began to fall down my cheeks, but I felt a sense of sadness.

"I owe you so much, but first I want to apologize for everything I ever did to you, for all the hurtful things I've said about you, and for the pain I caused you. You saved my life last night, did you know that? And before I get mad at you because in some ways, I wanted to die, I just need you to know how sorry I am for everything." She said sincerely.

I thought about when Nevaeh gave up drinking and how some people threw her out of their homes. I wasn't going to throw this relationship away. Maybe it would never be the same, but I was going to forgive and keep the demons from entering this room. I would cause no fear for anyone. Just understanding.

"I don't know what to say, but I do forgive you. You were my best friend in elementary school, and you really hurt me, but I probably hurt you too. I'm so sorry Sarah, please don't die. I would miss you." I reassured her.

We both cried. We were grieving, perhaps, about how we were when we were little girls. We began remembering the smiles and the laughter that we shared in elementary school. We talked about Hope and the drawings that we made for her. There were sad and happy feelings, and suddenly, I could see the light on our canvasses. It made sense what Tim had told me about when light is finally revealed through years of colorful feelings.

"I'm going into treatment, again, Mary Grace. I've been in and out of treatment centers every summer for the last two years. I don't know if I can get clean. It's so hard, but I just wanted you to know that I think about you sometimes, and I'm so glad you have Tim. I miss you."

"I miss you too. And I believe in you. You are going to make it this time. I know you will be okay." I said.

I remembered to make good memories that morning, and they were being made. Sarah and I never became best friends again, but for those moments we spent in the hospital room, it was enough.

After that night, we were able to talk and smile and even laugh at times. The problem with becoming close friends again were the drugs she battled. They had taken over and had become her coping skill. She could not let them go. Tim and I prayed for her, and we knew when she was ready to *see* the colors in her life, the anger, the sadness, and the fear, she would *understand* the light on her canvas. With God, everything is possible, including turning an addiction into a victory. Nevaeh taught me that there were better ways to deal with our past and those ways did not include alcohol or drugs. I knew in my heart that Sarah and I forgave each other that morning. We had finally let go of the past and let God remind us of the memories we made when we were young. God saw Sarah as fearful and wonderful, and one day, I knew he would lead her out of the temptation of drugs. She would be healed.

13

There are three who testify, and they are one.

Life is defined by our experiences. Some of our daily practices we think are normal, but they are in fact, destructive. Triangles are destructive, but the Father, Son, and Holy Spirit bring defeat to the broken hearted!

I will never forget the night that my sister, Mary Bella, "escaped" from her abusive husband. Together they had a daughter, my niece Sheri, and when she walked into our home, she had black eyes and a busted lip. I didn't hardly recognize her anymore because her husband beat her up regularly. She fell in love her senior year in high school with Jermaine, who was a womanizer and very good looking. I couldn't understand why he would say he loved her and then beat her up so badly that she had become unrecognizable. The first time he beat her, my mom told her that it was normal and that she just needed to work harder to be a better wife, whatever that meant.

My dad drank and sometimes didn't make the best decisions. However, not even drinking was an excuse to hit a woman. My dad never hit my mom, even though he did yell at her sometimes. Mary

Bella was told over and over again not to be yoked to a nonbeliever, but she didn't listen. Nevaeh told me there was no reason to hit a woman, none whatsoever! Even a man who doesn't believe in God should never mistreat a woman.

Nevaeh told me that domestic violence was about power and control. She said she had once gone to a church sermon where the minister was talking about these very things. She gave me a piece of paper.

"I will be right back."

When Nevaeh returned, she had a notebook. "I take notes when I go to church, and I put them in my healing basket because church services always cheer me up."

She opened up the notebook. "Where is that page? Oh, here it is."

She continued, "Okay, Mary Grace, draw a triangle."

She paused as I drew a triangle. "Now write 'bad guy' on the top, 'victim' on the bottom left, and 'rescuer' on the bottom right."

I did this. "This is how we, as human beings make sense of our lives, of our families, and even any of our systems. We have to put a label on everything and everyone to understand ourselves and others. However, we make a huge mistake by putting God in this same triangulation. God, thankfully doesn't think like us."

"Now I want to draw another triangle. This time I want you to write G-O-D in the middle of the triangle. On the top of the triangle I want you to write 'God,' on the left hand side write 'Jesus' and on the right hand side write 'Holy Spirit.'"

After I wrote these down, I looked at each triangle and noticed 'bad guy' was in the same place as 'God,' 'victim' was in the same place as 'Jesus' and 'rescuer' was in the same place as 'Holy Spirit.'

"So, is God a 'bad guy' for allowing his son to die on the cross?" I asked.

"Not at all, Mary Grace." Nevaeh explained. "This is how people see God, but it is because this is how we see ourselves. God made us in his image. Yet, man creates God in his image. It's a contradiction of who God really is. The difference between these two triangles is that G-O-D is in the middle of the second triangle. He is God, he is Jesus, and he is the Holy Spirit."

"Oh, the trinity." I tried to understand.

"Well, there is no word for 'trinity' in the Bible, so I think this is why people get confused. It's a man-made assumption that God resembles man. No, no, no. The truth is, we resemble God. As human beings, we get caught up in all kinds of triangles, with our families, friends, and even in our workplaces. God is not bad for allowing his son to die on the cross because Jesus *is* God. God allowed himself to suffer so we could have a relationship with him, the ultimate sacrifice that we would understand if we stopped making God to be the 'bad guy.' The Holy Spirit is also God, and when Jesus was talking about Mark 3:28, when the Pharisees were referring to Jesus as an 'evil spirit,' this is what they meant about a sin against the Spirit that cannot be forgiven. When we think of God as evil, a 'bad guy,' we are acting like the Pharisees. We have to remember that God is good and holy. He didn't exactly rescue us, as we define 'rescuer.' Our idea of 'rescuer' is someone or something that makes us feel better. Things like drugs, alcohol, and hurting someone can become our rescuer, although destructive, and they do make people feel better. God, on the other hand, is our savior, someone who *rescues* us from harm. This is what God means when he says that our troubles are only temporary. He has already rescued us from harm, as long as we make the decision to follow him. Otherwise, we can be deceived by a triangle of labeling, blaming, and placating. We must stop seeing others as victims but rather as victors. Encourage your family to look to God and not the storms, to allow him to rescue them from harm, not becoming the rescuer just to feel better, and to have confidence that God will help them as long as they make him the central part of their triangle, understanding that he is God, Jesus, and the Holy Spirit!"

"This reminds me of a book I was reading by Dr. Henry Morris in my gifted class for science." I began. "Interesting, he said the entire universe is Trinitarian. It's made up of matter, space, and time. Matter is made up of mass, energy, and motion. Space is length, height, and breadth. Time is the past, present, and future. Matter, space and time could not exist without each other or without what they are made up of. God exists as himself, as Jesus, and as the Holy Spirit. His existence is not out of our ideas, although we put him in our triangle and sometimes see him as a 'bad guy.' Wow, Nevaeh, can you imagine the possibilities of our lives if we saw ourselves in God's triangle? We would not see ourselves as victims or even question why God allows us to go through hardships. Instead, we would be one with God, realizing that the Holy Spirit is within us, and so we walk with God, not away from him, and we see Jesus as the example of *how* to live, by the fruit of the spirit."

"Exactly! And the fruit of the spirit is love, joy, peace, patience, kindness, goodness, faithfulness, gentleness, and self-control. In my opinion, I think God gave us the Holy Spirit so we could experience something invisible taking on a visible effect. Jesus had this attitude, and he wasn't a victim. God came as a man, and he demonstrates faith, hope, love, and kindness. He also shows us what we are capable of doing if we are led by our own understanding. Our triangles result in hatred, disobedience, manipulation, and even power and control. We are rescued by our own demise sometimes, but I'd rather be saved by God, even when I feel like a victim. Jesus wasn't a victim. He proves that obedience to God results in victory. I want to be victorious in every situation!"

"Me too!" I said enthusiastically.

Nevaeh made God real to me. He wasn't some man in heaven or far away. He was our daddy, our best friend, our hero, and he was the center of our lives. God made our families win, so everyone could win. There were no losers, just people choosing to be rescued by things that made them feel good. God went further by saving us from harm, which may not always make us feel better. Jesus, who we strive to imitate, went through so much and endured pain to save us from harm. I was gaining confidence in faith and hope and in love.

I looked at my family system. My brother Solomon drank frequently with our dad. John started to drink too, but he stopped after he married his wife and they had twin girls. John told me that he stopped drinking because he witnessed how destructive it was to dad, to mom and to their marriage. He turned to God because God was the only one who could help him. Nevaeh's explanation of man's point of view versus God's reality made sense as I looked at my family tree. John had come to the realization that he wasn't going to blame anyone for his bad mistakes. He let God be his savior from harm, and he kept God in the center of his life. He had a good wife, and my twin nieces were the cutest little girls. They were full of personality and very talented at singing. I saw them at church every Sunday in their pretty little dresses, always looking like angels but their big brown eyes and sneaky little smiles told me another story. I could tell they had my brother wrapped around their fingers, but Loren was a very strict mom, and every time she would catch their eyes, they would sit up and even cross their legs like little ladies. They would call me auntie and ask for cookies, being very disappointed when I didn't bring some to church. I rarely disappointed them because they were so cute and grateful. I was so glad that John was not repeating the mistakes our parents made and I always wished him my best. I knew one day our family would be reconciled. I had faith they would all be healed from the unhealthy rescuers in their lives. Only God is the true Savior!

Ruth, my other sister, had become a teacher. We weren't surprised because she loved school, and she went to college on scholarships while working her way through school at a dental office, filing and working the front desk, part time. In high school, she graduated top of class and had a 4.0 in college. My dad would call her his little "profesora," professor. She lived alone and went on many hikes and bike rides. She didn't own a car and lived just a few blocks from the elementary school, which is where she taught 3rd grade. We sometimes picked her up on Sundays to go to church. Otherwise, she would ride her bike, nearly five miles, to church. She told me she liked her independence and she enjoyed exploring her surroundings. One night, when I stayed the night at her house, she opened up to me, which she rarely ever did.

"I'll never get married." She said. "Mom and dad made marriage seem like a chore, so I'll never do it."

It is true that they had a difficult marriage, but I, on the other hand, romanticized marriage. Maybe it was because of the stories

Nevaeh told me about her parents. People could be happy, I thought, if you found the right person.

"Perhaps one day you'll change your mind." I told my sister.

"Nope. I've already decided I will never get married. Besides, I'm already married to God." She replied, and I believed her because once Ruth made up her mind about something, that was a done deal.

My little sister Esther was still charming her way through school. She had won President of her class every year since 7th grade. All the boys liked her, but not the way they liked Mary Bella. All the boys wanted to get into Mary Bella's pants. If Esther even felt somewhat disrespected by a boy, she would tell them off and use tactics that made them afraid to look at her that way again. The girls liked her too, but I think they were scared to death of her. She had a way of turning others against you, so the girls remained on her good side. I'm not sure how Esther was able to keep such a good balance, and keep so many friends, but probably from watching all of us, her siblings, and learning from our mistakes.

I finally thought about Mary Bella. On this particular night, when we saw her with black eyes and a scratched face, my dad picked up his gun and told her to leave him.

"I should go over there, man to man, and shoot him myself." My dad told Mary Bella.

"Dad, I don't need more drama in my life, and I don't need to lose you too!" She screamed.

My mom just gazed into my dad's eyes, like she was telling him something, to change the triangulation that caused us to become victims instead of victors.

"Just leave him, mi jita." My mom surprisingly said.

"But I love him. I *need* him so much, and we have a child together." Mary Bella responded desperately.

"Love is not supposed to hurt this much." My mom spoke from experience. "You can live with us, and no, you don't need him. This is always your home."

"You are living a death sentence and Jesus already died for us and for all of our sins." I interjected, because I didn't want her to go back to an empty vessel.

Mom and Mary Bella looked at me, not knowing what to say. I had left them speechless.

"Could you please not get involved in my business Mary Grace?" Mary Bella, annoyed at me, asked.

"I'm sorry, but I can't stay silent and watch you and my niece go through this anymore. Either you stop seeing yourself as a victim and get up and leave him or you should just go home and not come here every time he beats you. If you want to be a casualty, then go back, but if you want to come closer to God and be safe from harm, stay here." I spoke up.

Mary Bella began to cry. "You're right, Mary Grace. I can't live like this anymore."

She fell asleep in my mom's arms, crying. I went to bed and slept with Sheri, who was already fast asleep. I looked at her little face and kissed her forehead. I was glad I spoke up because I had to do what I could to protect my niece from growing up and witnessing her dad beat her mom. I didn't want Sheri to see her mom as a target or her dad as a bad guy, and who knows what Sheri might find to rescue her? It could be bad, or it could be the same thing she had been witnessing.

I slept through the night, holding on to Sheri. Before I dozed off, I prayed that God would help my sister and Sheri find God in the center of their lives. I asked for them to be free from the violence, and I didn't want them to continue this death sentence. Sometimes God does answer prayers because the next day they decided to never go back to a home where love didn't exist. They stayed with us. Mary Bella would now break free and become the woman that God had wanted her to be, not a victim. I prayed that the Holy Spirit would guide her. Besides, God was her protector, and he would mend her broken heart. Jesus would sustain her. She was more than a conqueror, never to be separated from the deity of God.

CHAPTER

14

Nothing is impossible with God.

*Until death do us part is a vow that married
people take but don't often keep. I realize life
has been difficult for both of you. There is no
guarantee that you will fulfill your vows to one
another, but I will fulfill my vow to both of
you. I will love you both until my last breath.*

In November of my senior year, my parents became separated.
Mary Bella was working on becoming a paralegal and had been
hired by three partners, attorneys, who paid her well. Our mom was
helping her with Sheri and our dad's drinking had taken a toll on
everyone in our household, so my dad moved in with Solomon, who
was single, again. Solomon had a hard time keeping a job.

My dad got him a job with the construction company, where
my dad was a foreman. My dad made more money than most people there considering he had no formal education. He had earned a
G.E.D. years after he dropped out of high school, which was enough
to earn him his current position.

This was a very difficult time for me and Esther, although
Esther took it harder than me. She became more withdrawn, but I
would not let her lose her feisty spirit.

"It is your spirit, little sissy, that is going to get you through this." I told her on the bus one morning as she left to school in tears.

Tim kept looking over the bus seat at us. He wanted to add some words of encouragement, but could find none.

"Are mom and dad trying to ruin the rest of my high school experience?" She asked me.

"No. They just need to be apart to work on some things." I answered her. "Don't take it personally. Mom and dad have always had problems. Let them work through this and maybe, just maybe, they will get back together."

When we arrived at school, Esther looked at me and sarcastically said, "Well, by the time they decide to get back together, I'm going to like them being apart, so they can play their little games. Quite frankly, I don't care anymore."

Tim looked up at her from his seat, "You do care, and God will heal their marriage. God is good Esther!"

Esther rolled her eyes. Her friends were surrounding her, and they all got off the bus, consoling her. I was glad she had her friends because at least they would distract her from thinking about mom and dad.

Tim and I got off the bus, and he said, "She'll be okay Mary Grace. I know you always defend your little sister, but she needs to surrender this to the good Lord!"

"Yes, she does! I know she can dramatic, but it's not even easy for her or for me to think about our parents being separated." I said. "I wish my dad would get some help. He's never even tried."

"Let's go by and talk to Nevaeh." Tim said. "She always has the best advice."

School seemed to go by slowly this day. I was doing very well and was going to graduate valedictorian if I kept up my grades. I was under so much pressure because the salutatorian was one tenth of a point behind me. My sister Ruth had been the salutatorian, and everyone made a big deal out of it since no one in my family had graduated with such high honors. Our parents had not even graduated from high school. Solomon and John were the first in our family to get a high school diploma. Ruth had done so well, and even Mary Bella graduated in the top ten percent of her class, so our parents were very happy with how they did in high school. They had even higher hopes for me and Esther. I worked hard in high school, and I also prayed every night to do well in school. I needed all the help I could get.

I let Esther know that Tim and I would get off the bus at the stop closer to Nevaeh's house. For the first time ever, she wanted to go visit Nevaeh with us.

When we arrived at Nevaeh's, she was expecting us. She had made extra beans and chili, just in case we were hungry. She had already called my mom and Tim's mom to let them know.

"I'll call your mom and inform her that Esther is also safe with me." She said when she saw us at the front door.

While Nevaeh called our mom, we took off our coats and went into the bathroom to wash our hands and freshen up. We were all starving and the beans and chili smelled so good.

We sat down to eat, and Nevaeh blessed our food. She didn't eat with us because she had eaten earlier and wasn't hungry. She told us she would have frozen the beans and chili if we hadn't shown up.

"I know you've been distraught, Mary Grace about your parents, so I expected you'd come and see me. When you finish your food, I have something to share from my healing basket. Take your time eating, and Tim, take another tortilla." She said as Tim had already eaten one tortilla and seemed to want another one but was afraid to get one.

"Thank you Nevaeh." Tim said graciously. "I barely ate lunch today. I'm starving!"

She gave him some more beans and chili, but I was full with the first serving, so I didn't take seconds. Esther ate about half of her food, but that was typical of her. She didn't eat as much as the rest of us at home. My dad said it was because she was the baby of the family and had to learn to survive on little food. I just think she was a picky eater, but she used my dad's statement to her advantage and my mom made sure she was fed well.

After we finished eating, we put the dishes in the sink and Nevaeh said she would wash them later. She had us rinse them so they would be easier to wash.

Nevaeh had her healing basket in the living room on the coffee table. She had us sit down while she pulled out an acorn out of her basket, which she kept in a plastic bag.

"When I first started going to Alcoholics Anonymous, A.A., I moved quickly through the first three steps. Step one was to admit I was powerless over my addiction. Easy, I was powerless. The second step was to believe a power greater than ourselves restores us to sanity. I believed that then, and I still believe that now, even though I was wrestling with God in so many ways. Third, we made a decision to turn our lives over to God. I got stuck on this one because I had no idea who God was at that time. I mean, a few people who attended A.A. didn't even believe in God, so they made a coffee can that represented God and put everything in there, the inventory, their wrongs, and their defects of character. I was so angry at God. I still believed in him, but I was mad at him. I didn't believe in his power. I even felt hatred towards God. I mean, why God allowed my mom to die, I thought, was something I could never comprehend. So, I decided to find my "god," and one day in the fall, while I was taking a walk, I found this acorn, from my old oak tree. I began turning all of my hatred, my anger, my pain, my sorrow, and my anguish to this acorn. You see, it was no longer a part of the tree. In fact, it was dead. This is exactly how I felt, dead inside. There was this huge void in my heart, and I couldn't let it go. During the Holidays, we had an A.A. party. In A.A., we have sponsors who keep us accountable for our sobriety. We can call our sponsors if we start struggling or we need support. To this day, I have my sponsor, and I still attend the meetings every other week. My sponsor told me the night of the party if I was ready to make an inventory of all my wrongs, but I just couldn't. I went home after the party and wanted to get drunk. I wanted to taste the alcohol that had made me feel better. I took the acorn and threw it against the wall and began yelling at God. I begged him to take me out of this world. I was so full of hatred. I took the Bible and threw it across the table. As I sat on the floor in my living room crying and yelling at God, I heard a loud noise. To this day I've never figured out what it was that I heard, but it made me calm down, at least enough to see the Bible on the floor. I turned the Bible over and right there in front of me was this scripture. She removed a piece of paper from the plastic bag containing the acorn. Psalm 22:1-4 reads, 'My God, my God, why hast thou forsaken me? Why art thou so far from helping me, and from the words of my roaring? O my God, I cry in the day time, but thou hearest not; and in the night season, and am not silent. But thou art holy, O thou that inhabitest the praises of Israel. Our fathers trusted in thee: they trusted, and thou didst deliver them.'" Nevaeh paused, as to hold her breath, and she felt emotional.

She continued, with tears in her eyes, "Suddenly, like the loud noise I had heard, I had also listened to God. I did not trust him because I blamed him for the anguish, and so I felt he had abandoned me. That night I made a decision to let God deliver me from this dark pit that I was trapped in. I asked him to help me see the light at the end of the tunnel. I know it sounds cliché, but that is what I needed, and he delivered. After that night, I became a different person inside. I was a sober woman. I no longer had to depend on alcohol to cope with my mom's death. This is when I started putting all my memories in this healing basket. Perhaps, in a way, it became my "temple." It became a place where I could surrender all the pain and all the sadness and even all the anger towards God. People who were my drinking buddies told me I had changed after that night. They saw a peace in my demeanor, but they also told me I had become more serious. Every person I ever drank with no longer could enjoy my company because they said I was not any fun anymore. The reason I'm telling you all of this is because I talked to my sponsor and to your mom about doing an intervention with your dad and brother Solomon. Sometimes the healthiest person in the family is the one who seems the most sick."

Tim interrupted Nevaeh, "What? How can someone who drinks be the healthiest one in the family? That makes no sense."

"I don't know your dad very well, girls, and what he does is not healthy. I'm not saying that at all. Solomon, on the other hand, has followed in his footsteps, and I've heard you tell me he's a mess. Well, in a way, he is just a reflection of the family system practicing unhealthy coping skills. Let me clarify, it is the reflection that is healthy, not the individual. The reflective part is healthy because when we look in the mirror, we can take an inventory of how we look. We can brush our hair if it's messy or wash our faces if it's dirty. We can change our clothes if they don't look good on us. It is the same with the family system. When you see Solomon, he is just reflecting what is happening in your family, the alcoholism of your dad, the people that he has hurt as a result of his drinking, and even the things he says that are hurtful to his family and friends. These are the destructive ways of dealing with life. Now that we see them clearly, we can change them, but the entire system has to change. Even you girls will be impacted and may have to change some things. So, a lot of chaos will come out of this, but you have to be part of the solution, not part of the problem. When you hear your brother or your dad start talking about their lives, don't take it personally, especially if they blame your mom or even one of you for some of the issues. We all have our perspectives about life. My sponsor tells me that family members who grew up in the same family grow up with different perceptions of what happened and with different values. Being different is not a bad thing. However, building our convictions on the word of God is the only thing that will give us healing. Remember this as we do this intervention. It may work for both of them or it may work for neither one of them. Just remember that God has not forsaken you or your family. Listen to him when he speaks and let yourselves be led by the holy spirit."

No matter what happened, I thought, I would love both of my parents. Solomon will always be my brother, and regardless what he reflected in the mirror, I would show him love too. Nevaeh always told me that love never fails, so to my parents and my brother, I'd be kind and patient. I would not hold their shortcomings against them. I would be part of the solution.

Nevaeh gave us some bread as we put our coats and gloves on. The snow was beginning to fall again. I looked up at the old oak tree as we walked past it. I knew God was not an acorn, nor was my dad and brother. God *is* the tree, and my dad and brother are still alive somewhere in those branches. I kept silent as I listened to God tell me this. As we continued walking, I knew God was speaking to me.

CHAPTER

15

Be steadfast with your feelings as the sun go down.

There are many songs written about feelings. Some people say feelings are overrated. But are they, really? They can mend a broken heart, they can fix a sick family, and they can help validate a broken spirit, as long as we are not deceived by our feelings.

"Mary Grace," Tim said as we walked to the bus after school in the spring. "I knew you could do it!"

I wasn't supposed to know, but it was the last six weeks of our senior year, and I would be graduating "numero uno," number one in my class! There was no way Jennifer Hace would be able to catch up with me anymore. Even if she received straight A's, and I got a B, I'd still beat her. My grades were all high A's, and the lowest my grades could go were low A's, if I failed the finals, which I never did. I would have to stop going to school or doing my work if my grades were to come down, but I'd make sure this wouldn't happen.

Tim was working in the office as a student aide, and he had the inside scoop about who got suspended and whose parents had visited the principal, although he did not tell me much because he said gossip was not a good thing. He was apprised of all the scholarship recipients and the now the top ten seniors, and I was the valedictorian. This, he could not keep a secret from me. It was an honor for me, and for my family. I would have to give the valedictory speech at the graduation ceremony.

My parents were back together, and my dad was going to A.A. every week, sometimes two times a week. An A.A. group had been started in our church, and many people had overcome this demon. He had a very good sponsor, a leader in our church who I was surprised was an alcoholic. His sponsor was a local business owner, Frank Martin, who owned the largest automobile dealership and several auto repair shops in our community. He lived in a beautiful ranch house outside our village. He had reconciled his marriage, and they had one little boy. He invited us all over for dinner sometimes, after he started sponsoring dad, and he told us his alcoholism was the cause for his failed marriage, but God had saved him and had become the glue that keeps him together with his wife. He and his wife often said they wouldn't still be together without God. His wife gave God the glory and told us that he led her husband towards sobriety…and then back to her, and she thanked God every day for a new husband.

"God has a way of making our old selves new. I don't recognize Frank anymore, and I am so grateful to God for this life!" she said.

Frank told dad to count his blessings because mom could have left him many years ago. Mom attended her own meetings, Al-Anon, for Christian women and families married to or children of alcoholics. I sometimes went to these meetings with mom, and my siblings also attended the meetings. The meetings were Christ-centered, and listening to other people's testimonies made us realize the power of God. He was the changing agent in our lives. My dad became the man I always saw, the man God had created perfectly.

Solomon had a difficult time kicking the habit, although he seemed to be holding a job. Nevaeh often referred to him as a "functional alcoholic." She said he used to not be able to hold a job, and at least now, he was somewhat functional, which, she explained, showed progress. He would remain sober at times and then binge drink, but we prayed for him every day, and we knew God would heal him, just as he had healed my dad. I would often look at Solomon as a reflection of our family and realized that in some ways, we had done this to him. He was carrying all the things that we had taught him, the drinking, the avoidance, the rescuing, and the struggles with healthy communication skills. I tended to avoid my family, and Nevaeh said this wasn't always healthy. She told me there were some things that were much better to walk away from, but there were other things we should confront, like why my mom got mad at me for telling her of the scary experience I had as a child when my dad was drunk. She said family secrets were not a good coping skill and I had the right to talk about things that bothered me. She said we had to forgive and move forward, but it's hard to move on when we keep things in the darkness. God can heal us when we live in the light.

Sometimes my family called me "temperamental" because I would get so frustrated with the fighting in my household. After Nevaeh told me that it was my temperament that helped me survive through some of the fighting, I felt validated. She said she'd be worried if I didn't get angry, but I had to look in the mirror and find better ways to deal with my anger. Avoidance was one of those way, which caused me to eat in secret. I was the heaviest one in my family, and it was because I ate my anger away. Another way I dealt with my anger was by slamming the doors and leaving the house, always finding my way to Nevaeh's home.

"Where would you go if I wasn't here?" Nevaeh asked me one day.

"I'd go to Tim's house." I answered her.

"What if his parents didn't welcome you?" She asked me another question.

I began crying. "Don't you want me here? Am I a burden here too?"

Nevaeh gave me a hug, but I was stiff. I didn't want her to touch me because I felt she didn't want me there.

She handed me a Kleenex. "Of course, you are always welcomed here. I just asked you that question to make a point. When you become mad at something your family member does, you slam doors and leave. They know you're mad, but you don't say anything. I just want you to learn to tell people how you feel. Tell them that you're angry. Say it out loud, and if they try to keep you from expressing those feelings, let them know that you wish they would listen to how you feel, and then if you need to come to my house, I'll be here waiting. There is nothing wrong with taking a break from people. Just don't leave in a rage of anger. God wants us to be resolved. Leave in peace, and when you return, love them."

"Well, Nevaeh, you made me…"

She interrupted me, "Say how you feel, not how I made you feel. Start with 'I feel,' because I don't have the power to make you feel anyway, unless you give it to me."

"*I feel* angry that you don't want me here." I practiced.

"I do want you here. I just don't want you to keep your feelings in anymore, and I'm sorry how you feel. You are always welcomed here." Nevaeh said.

"Right now, I don't feel welcomed." I told her.

Nevaeh responded, "That's okay that you feel that way, but I want you to hear me. Listen. I want you here. You are always welcomed."

I believed her this time. After she said that I am always welcomed, we prayed. Nevaeh said it is important to pray after you deal with your feelings. Feelings can be deceitful, and we had to be led by the spirit, not our feelings.

Incredibly, I felt better. I would practice this new coping skill at home, but I knew my family didn't come across as understanding as Nevaeh. Nevaeh told me it was because I didn't live with her. She said all family systems had problems, and they needed to learn how to deal with life productively. She told me it was our direction that God cared about, not perfection.

Nevaeh went to her healing basket and had some index cards. She read them to me. "These are my feelings to different people, mostly to God. Here goes. God, I feel, angry that you allowed my dad and mom to die so young, but I am so blessed, knowing you can handle my anger."

That was just on the first index card. She turned it over. "I wish you had allowed them to stay with me longer. I need for you to help me through this journey because I feel depressed sometimes."

She read the next index card. "Mom, I feel sad that you are no longer with me. I feel lonely without you."

She turned it over. "I need for you to know how much I love you and appreciate all the little things you did for me. I'm sorry for taking you for granted. I miss you."

"Dad, I feel so heartbroken that you left me so young, but I am so proud that you are a hero, you are my hero." She read the third index card and when she turned it over, she said, "I need for you to take care of mom in heaven. Give Estevan a kiss on the cheek for me. Hugs to you."

"I wrote another feeling for God. It's about you, so hear, not just listen, to what I say about you when you aren't here. God, I feel so hopeful and joyful when you bring people like Mary Grace in my life. I really need more people who help me see you more clearly. Thank you, Father for your constant support and reassurance that you are in my life!"

"It's okay to have more than one feeling about someone. We just can't allow ourselves to be deceived." She finished.

There were many index cards, but Nevaeh only shared these four. She said the rest were private, and she would feel uncomfortable sharing any more with me.

She went to one of her kitchen drawers and handed me a stack of index cards, saying, "Now it's your turn to write down how you feel on one side of the card, and on the back of the card, write down what you need from that person. Sometimes we can't tell them directly what we need because they are no longer here with us, but we can still say it."

I spent the rest of the afternoon writing down what I felt for dad, mom, and all my siblings. I wrote down how I felt towards Tim and then Sarah. I told them all what I needed from them. When I got to the last index card, I told Nevaeh it was for her, and I wanted to share it.

I looked at her and smiled, saying, "I feel so happy when I think about you, Nevaeh. You are my best friend."

"I need for you to always remember how much I appreciate all you've done for me. I need you to know I wouldn't be where I am today if it wasn't for you. I need you to know that I love you!" I wrote on the back of the card.

Nevaeh began to cry, and this time I hugged her and whispered, "You are the best friend I've ever had. I really need you, period."

We smiled at one another, wiped our tears, went to the living room, and she opened the top of her record player. She took the Saturday Night Fever album and played our song, *More Than a Woman.*

We danced the rest of the afternoon, until my mom called for me to come home. When I came home, I placed the index cards in my healing basket. Now I could express my feelings without slamming doors or without eating when I was hurt. I would quietly turn to God and pray. No one could take my feelings away from me, but God was the reason my feelings would not deceive me. He was the one who would validate me. I could let go of negative perceptions and trust that God would increase my joy...and I would no longer let the sun go down when I was angry.

"I promise, God," I whispered.

CHAPTER

16

Plans to prosper us, and plans to give us a future.

I will find something I love, make a career out of it and never work a day in my life. Life is too short to work a job that brings us unhappiness. I choose to be happy with my chosen career.

"Class of 1985, future graduates, parents, administrators, teachers, and distinguished guests. Like our school song begins, 'Tonight's the night we make history…' Our history began our freshmen year, when the girls wore high heels and boys sported ties to try and impress the upperclassmen. After that first day, we realized t-shirts, Levis and tennis shoes were a much better choice and more comfortable. I'll only say this once and never again, but, mom, you told me so! As sophomores, we were just glad not to be freshmen anymore. We were beginning to come up in rank, many of us made Varsity sports or we joined a club that gave us notoriety. By the time we were juniors, we began to make mistakes. Some of the errors were lessons learned, like when four students, whose names I will not mention--Jesus, Martin, Lucas, and Tommy--started a fire in Chemistry class. They were great educational moments, not because of what they did, and let me add, it was not on purpose, but because no one else in our class every put papers near the burners after that incident. We all know to keep them away from the flames. Our Chemistry teacher told us that how many times? Finally, we understand why. We had a lot of fun when we went on trips out of town. We were regional champions in football, took state in cheerleading, and many of our music students went to state competitions. We had some regional science fair winners and all of our Varsity teams brought home a trophy. I can see most of our teachers wiping their foreheads because thankfully, nothing bad ever happened. You can breathe more easily now. Well, at least until next year. Some of our memories were not so good. We lost people who touched our lives. We were defeated at times, but these things did not break our spirit. Finally, we entered our senior year. These have been the best of times and these have been the worst of times. Some days we were hit with storms and other days with sunshine, just as the song continues. From this day forward, we will choose our careers, we will make other mistakes, we will make good choices, and we will make history. To accomplish greatness, we must not only act but also dream; not only plan but also believe! This is not just our motto, this is our future. Congratulations class! We made it to graduation day!"

Tim ran up to me after the commencement ceremony and gave me a great big hug. He was so proud of my speech, since I had practiced it in front of him and Nevaeh several times. Some people had mixed feelings about my speech, but Tim told me we couldn't please everyone all the time, and he was right. I was sad that Tim and I would be parting ways soon. We had all kinds of plans after high school, but things had changed. He would be leaving in a few days to a Christian college and major in Theology. He wanted to be a minister and had earned a full ride scholarship through our church. He would get his education paid as long as he maintained a 2.5 grade point average.

I had received many scholarships to college but decided to attend a community college and become a chef. Everyone, and I do mean everyone, seemed surprised, but this was my career choice, and I was excited about it. I mean, I was already selling my baked goods for a profit. I had catered a few small events for Frank Martin's dealership, so I was making a name for myself. More like God was blessing my career choice. I had many events planned for the summer, even a small wedding, and was baking like crazy for graduation parties.

I would be attending the community college in Albuquerque, New Mexico in the fall and was very excited. I would be living by myself in an apartment and received enough grant money to be financially independent. I told Nevaeh I would come visit her at least twice a month, and I kept my promise to her.

After our high school ceremony, Nevaeh threw me a little get together, as she called it, at her house. All of my family was there. It was the first time since I was a little girl that we all were together at the same time. It was a great day, and we all got along. My mom and dad looked happy, and my little sister, who was doing well in school also, told me she had big shoes to fill. I received a lot of money from my family, $552.00, but the most amazing gift was from Nevaeh.

She gave me a box, wrapped in gold. I thought it was jewelry at first.

"Listen everyone," she said. "I have known Mary Grace since she was in elementary school, so I consider her my second daughter. Lily, if you could please join me."

Lily walked to her mom and stood next to her. I rarely saw Lily, but I was so excited that she had made plans to visit her mom during my graduation.

"I have a healing basket." Nevaeh began. "Mary Grace has listened while I shared stories of souvenirs I've kept in the basket, so today, I am sharing another story. After my mom passed away, I received an insurance policy, which as many of you know, I went through to help Estevan when he was sick. I also received something else, and I am giving it to Mary Grace. Open up the box."

When I opened the box, there were keys to a 1958 Chevy Biscayne. I was speechless.

"This is too generous." I said. "I can't take it."

Lily responded. "Please take it! I have to drive it every time I come visit, and it's a standard, and we've already had to replace the clutch once. It only has 2,500 miles on it, and I had to get my mom some cats to keep the mice out of her barn. The rats were beginning to chew through the wires, so we had to fix that too. It's become a money pit for us. I will never take it to Mississippi. I'd probably burn out the clutch between here and there, so I reassured my mom I didn't want it. We have prayed about it, and we want you to have it. This is a blessing from God. Remember that."

"Well, if you put it that way, of course I'll take it. Thank you!" I said gratefully.

Everyone was in awe of Nevaeh's gift to me. I loved driving standards. My dad had a standard truck, and I had been driving it since I was 13 years old on the ranch, but sometimes he let me take it to school when he wasn't working, which was very rare.

Nevaeh had given Tim some money, $100.00, and he was happy with that, even though he said a car was even better. He didn't complain because he knew how close I had become to Nevaeh over the years.

When the party was over, Tim and I stayed to help Nevaeh clean her house. We vacuumed and mopped while Nevaeh and Lily washed all the dishes.

"I told you, mom, to buy paper plates and plastic forks and spoons." We heard Lily telling Nevaeh.

"Stop nagging me Lily. That's my job, to nag you." Nevaeh responded.

Lily stuck her tongue out, and Nevaeh bumped her with her hips. We could tell they were very close, and I loved the way they talked to each other.

"Oh, my goodness!" Nevaeh said, "I haven't had that many people over since forever.

"Mom, you have used what God has given you to bless other people." Lily responded.

"I've taught you well, haven't I?" Nevaeh asked.

"You are an awesome mom! But next time take my advice and get paper plates and plastic spoons and forks, so we could spend more time together instead of washing dishes." She complained.

"I'm your mom! I tell you what to do, and besides, we are spending time together little girl," She responded.

We saw Nevaeh putting her arm around Lily as Lily washed the dishes and said. "Thank you for helping me, mi jita."

"You're welcome mama." Lily said.

When Tim and I completed the work she had given us, we gave Nevaeh and Lily a hug good-bye. We were so anxious to go cruising in my new car!

"Be safe." Nevaeh said as we closed the door behind us.

We drove to Tim's house for some cassette tapes. He had Christian music. He had more of a conviction about music than I did because I still liked the *Staying Alive* album. We both loved Amy Grant and Sandi Patti, but our favorite song was *One Day at a Time* by Christy Lane. If our classmates knew about our music, they would probably laugh, but what they thought didn't matter anymore. We imagined Jesus in the middle of the front seat singing with us.

On the boom box, we turned up the music as we drove through our village and then we drove on to the paved road, listening to music. We sang, "I'm only human. I'm just a man. Help me to believe in what I could be and all that I am. Show me the stairway that I have to climb. Lord for my sake teach me to take one day at a time. One day at a time sweet Jesus that's all I'm asking from you. Give me the strength to do every day what I have to do. Yesterday's gone sweet Jesus and tomorrow may never be mine. So for my sake teach me to take one day at a time..."

These were the best of times, times I will always remember, with my best friend. He made high school worth getting up for and doing well in school. He helped make good memories with me in high school fun. Now we would be going on different journeys. He would be a minister, and I would be a chef. I knew he would inspire others through his sermons, and I recognized working mine would be exhilarating. One day I would be doing exactly what I loved and would feel like I wasn't even working. But for now, we were making history, driving the car and jamming our music, with Jesus!

CHAPTER

17

Delight in God, and he will give you the desires of your heart.

Believe in your dreams. They can become reality. Believe in yourself. You can become anything. Believe in the power of healing, and you can overcome your biggest fears. Face all the things that hinder your dreams, and you will become your dreams.

After I graduated from high school, I left my small town to attend a Community College in Albuquerque, New Mexico. I wanted to be a chef and had plans to open my own restaurant. Nevaeh had taught me to cook delicious foods and to bake. I also loved to eat, which is why no boys were interested in me. I was too fat for them. My mom was very proud of my goals and told me I would one day meet a man who would appreciate me, so I didn't worry about being alone.

At the college I attended, I was always at the top of my class. While many of the students could cook well, I knew how to use a variety of spices and vegetables to create incredible tasting recipes. Everyone tried to follow my recipes, but they never tasted as good. I just had a way of adding a pinch of salt, oregano, onion, garlic, and even lemon to make the food taste perfect. I couldn't put some things in my recipes. Nevaeh had taught me tricks to cooking and baking that were impossible to teach to others because it took years to learn.

I attended the school for two years and always brought my new creations to Nevaeh to taste. She would tell me to add a pinch of this, or a cup of that to make it better, and I was wise to take her advice. Her mom had owned a restaurant, so she knew how to make food taste and smell so good.

One of my professors recommended that I enter a baking competition as my education came to a close. If I won, which was a long shot, I would win a $25,000 grant. I wanted to open my own restaurant and needed the money, so I entered the competition. I had remembered visiting Nevaeh one day, and she cut me a piece of her "secret recipe" coconut cream pie. It was delicious, so delicious in fact, that I had three pieces and went home with a stomach ache. I couldn't eat dinner that night, but could not get the taste out of my mind. For many weekends, Nevaeh had tried to teach me how to make the pie, but I could not do it, not until I memorized the recipe. I had no choice but to memorize Nevaeh's recipes. She did not write them down. She made pies by memory, which is how her mom taught her. When I made the coconut cream pie perfect that first time, everyone asked me to make them one, and they began paying me for baking. At first, I would just ask for the cost of the ingredients, but then people gave me extra money, so I started a little business, and Nevaeh was always happy to help me. When I finally made the coconut cream pie perfect, Nevaeh told me a story about her mom.

"I'm going to tell you the one big lie I told to my mom. She always had me on diets because I was chubby. I loved to eat. That was my favorite thing to do." Nevaeh began.

"One day, I told my mom I had a bake sale and needed a coconut cream pie because hers were the best. She made me that pie, but I didn't really have a bake sale. I just wanted to eat a piece, or two, or maybe half. I was tired of dieting." She continued.

"As I was waiting for the bus, I had eaten half of the pie. What I didn't anticipate was my mom coming back home, as she had forgotten some things on the counter. When she saw me and half of the pie gone, she made me eat the entire pie for lying." She said, giggling.

"My stomach hurt so badly that day, but I learned a valuable lesson. I never lied to my mom again, and she taught me how to make that coconut cream pie. Of course, I never ate another whole pie again!" She chuckled again while finishing her story.

As I cut into the coconut pie I had baked, Nevaeh asked me to look at her.

"When I made my first coconut cream pie, my mom had me cut into it and said it was a piece of heaven. So, now I say to you, Mary Grace, this is a piece of heaven. Enjoy!" She said.

We both enjoyed that piece of pie that day, and it was perfect.

After I entered the contest, and when I brought my coconut cream pie to the gala, the judges all came to meet me. It was the best coconut cream pie they had ever tasted. This was very exciting for me, but I was disappointed that this was just the first step to winning the money. At this point, I had only made it into the show. The show, which was local, would be seen by all my friends and family who owned a television. The requirements included that I had to make five coconut cream pies. I would be competing with seven other people who had also made it into the competition. We all had different creations and none of us had to share our recipes, but we did have to name them. I called mine "a piece of heaven." In the competition, there was a grandmother, several restaurant owners, and a chef from New York City. I didn't think it was fair to have someone from out of state compete with us locals. I was concerned that he had many years of experience. However, he had lived in New Mexico for three years and was a resident, which was one of the requirements. At the pre-competition, we had to bake cookies. I baked biscochitos, which was a New Mexican cookie that melted in your mouth. There were oatmeal cookies, chocolate chip cookies, pecan cookies, pinon cookies, and even a cookie made with Bacardi. The chef from New York made a snooker doodle cookie. I was horrified when my biscochitos were compared to his snooker doodle cookies. I didn't think they tasted at all alike, but the judges loved my cookies as much as they loved his. I knew he would become my biggest competitor.

"I tasted your biscochitos," he told me, with a great big grin and a New York accent. "They are delicious. I love them with coffee."

He sounded rather funny. I wanted to "cough" about his "coughee." I didn't say anything about his accent, but it was quite interesting.

"Thank you," I took notice of him. "Yours are good too, but mine are better."

He giggled and said, flirting, "You can bake for me any time, and yes, yours are tastier. They melted in my mouth."

He was average in height, about 5'8" and he must have weighed about 200 pounds. He wasn't fat, but he was overweight. I could tell he liked to eat too. I was only 5'1 and weighed 150 pounds, although I carried my weight well. Most people didn't believe I was 40 pounds overweight, perhaps because I had large breasts, a small waist, and large hips. My mom said I was the Marilyn Monroe de la Raza, of the race, the Hispanic race, that is.

In the next few days, I spent all my free time with Ted Haskin, the chef from New York. He and his father had owned a very successful business in Manhattan, near the Italian district, and had sold it for "a lot" of money after his dad died. He moved to New Mexico to live with his uncle, who married a Hispanic woman in a nearby town.

"My dad was a single father and raised me alone. He loved to cook and bake, so he opened a restaurant, where he could bring me. He was always concerned about my well-being and didn't want me to become a 'wise guy,' which were young men in our neighborhood who would gamble and hang around with the mobsters. My dad was Italian, but my mom was Jewish. She died in a boating accident when I was only three, which my dad never recovered from. I don't remember her. I only know her from stories that my family told me about. My dad never remarried, and I guess I got so busy working at his restaurant, I never had time to date. I still don't date much. We visited New Mexico many times with my uncle, his only brother, who loved the women here. His brother married Raquel Montoya and never went back home. He jokingly used to call her Raquel Welch, and she does resemble her, especially her body. Time has not aged her. My dad heard about the green chili, which he secretly had overnighted to his restaurant. Raquel told him how to make it tasty. He used the green chili for flavor, and this put his restaurant in the New York Times, receiving rave reviews from critics. Nine years ago, he had a heart attack, and since I was only in middle school, I could not run the business by myself, although I tried. Some of his employees helped me keep it open until I finished high school. They took turns watching over me until I was old enough to live alone. It was never the same without him, so, with the help of my uncle, I sold the business and moved to New Mexico. My dad and I had many good times here, visiting local restaurants and sightseeing, so I decided to move out here permanently, with my only living relative. I love the weather and the mountains. I miss the ocean, though." He told me.

I didn't want to interact with my competition, but he was very charming and interesting. He was an excellent conversationalist. He also had a sense of humor that made me laugh. He sort of reminded me of John Travolta, and I noticed he had a smile that made me blush.

The night before the competition, we all had dinner together. Ted and I sat next to each other and continued to talk.

"Here," I said.

"What is this?" He asked.

"I made you some fresh baked bread." I said.

"I have something for you, too, "he replied.

He took out a bouquet of mint and continued. "This is my favorite thing to use when baking, but just don't tell anyone I let you in on one of my baking secrets."

He laughed out loud at his own jokes. I could feel my face turning red because I didn't think he was as funny as he did. Yet, the fact that he could laugh at himself made the situation even more hilarious.

"I wondered what was in that bag," I said, my heart pounding.

"Thank you, Ted." I continued, smiling, "No one has ever shared their secret ingredients like this with me before."

He replied, "And no girl has ever had this effect on me, and it's not just your baking, although that is definitely a plus."

"Flattery will get you everywhere," I said, being embarrassed that I said exactly what I was thinking.

"I want to bake with you after the competition." He said.

"Um, maybe," I said, moving closer to him. "But just because I am willing to bake with you doesn't mean I will share all my secrets with you."

He looked at me and chuckled. He had big, beautiful blue eyes, like the morning sky. He also smiled with them, which made him more attractive. He additionally had long eyelashes and perfect eyebrows. His teeth were straight and white, and he had lips that I knew would drive me crazy because I could tell he would be an excellent kisser.

"Now, you're not going to make me nervous by your beauty before the competition, so I can let you win, are you?" He asked jokingly.

"It is one of my ulterior motives." I said. "And it is my baking that will make you nervous, so I'm not worried. I am going to beat you fair and square."

"My dad told me that a real lady would capture my heart through her baking. I think you're trying to steal my heart, not my recipes." He said smiling happily.

"I am that girl, and I will only take your heart if you give it to me willingly. I don't steal, although I might borrow your secret ingredients." I said, thinking it sounded corny.

He continued to smile, and just then, one of the promoters came up to welcome us to the final competition. Ted and I just kept looking into each other's eyes. I remembered when Nevaeh told me how her dad looked at her mom. Perhaps this is what she was talking about, I thought. I was crushing for this chef, this half-Italian man. He was my John Travolta. I'd be more than a woman to him any day of the week! Did I really think that? Shame on me! Pastor Salas would be quite disappointed! Tim, however, would tell me to keep it pure. I better listen to my best friend.

The next day, we would be baking all day and later in the afternoon, we would be competing for the grand prize. I was determined to win, although I would be happy for Ted if he beat me. I couldn't stop thinking about how he looked at me, and I pretended to bake the pies just for him. I made five coconut cream pies. I was so proud of them because when I saw all of the pies together, mine stood out. I knew I had a good chance to win by the looks of the pies, and I was hoping the taste would give me the edge to win first place. There was an apple pie, a cherry pie, a lemon meringue pie, a pecan pie, and Ted made a key lime pie. They all looked delicious.

After the judges tasted the pies, they chose the three best pies, all of whom would win cash prizes. It was the grandmother, who made the cherry pie, Ted, and me. The third place winner would get $5,000.00, the second place winner would get $10,000, and the first place winner would get $25,000 and a monthly spot on the local television show.

"This was a very close competition." The announcer said, "And all of these top three bakers are winners. However, we can only have one first-place winner."

The third place winner was the grandmother. She was so happy to win a cash prize, saying that her cherry pie was her great-grandmother's recipe. I walked closer to the announcer. Ted and I looked at each other and smiled. No matter what happened, I had met someone wonderful at this competition, and I would see him again outside of this competition. I was already the winner of my John Travolta!

"By a tenth of a point, the second place winner is...." The announcer paused. "Ted Haskin! This means that you, Mary Grace Martinez, are the first place winner of $25,000!"

Ted put his arms around me and gave me a great big hug.

"Congratulations!" He whispered, "You deserve to win and your bread was awesome!"

"Would you like to say anything?" The announcer asked me.

"I want to thank my friend and the best cooking teacher I have ever had, Nevaeh. If you're watching, 'a little piece of heaven' is the winner!" I said.

Everyone clapped, and the show came to an end.

"So, do you want to celebrate tonight?" Ted asked me.

"Are you asking me out on a date?" I answered with a question.

"Yes." He replied.

"I would if I didn't have a curfew!" I teasingly stated. "But I will break curfew just for you."

I winked and wrote down my address.

"Pick me up by eight, and don't be late or my Fairy Godmother might turn your car into a pumpkin." I said, laughing.

"Well then I'll just have to make pumpkin pie, but I won't be late because you are so much sweeter than a pumpkin pie." He replied with a chuckle.

I rushed home to my apartment, took a shower, and spent the rest of the evening trying to figure out what to wear. I was embarrassed to think that I had never really gone on a date. I mean, I had gone out to eat with several friends or I had gone to a few movies with a group of people, but I had not had a date, not ever. I was so nervous but excited that I was going out with John Travolta. Well, Ted wasn't John Travolta, but he was close enough! I chose a red dress and flat black shoes. It was a very flattering dress, showing just enough cleavage to be noticed but also leaving plenty of room for the imagination.

When I heard the knock on the door, I was putting on my shoes. I walked quickly to the door, and Ted was holding one of his pies.

"I made an extra one, just for you," he said.

"Dessert?" I asked.

He smiled and nodded, looking at me up and down, but trying not to make it obvious.

"You look nice." He said.

I noticed he was wearing a blue and white poke a dot tie and a white shirt.

"You look handsome tonight." I replied.

He blushed and so did I. I placed the pie down on my kitchen counter, put a clean kitchen towel over it, and we walked out the door, hand in hand.

Ted and I went out to dinner at a quaint little Mexican restaurant. He asked me if he could order several dishes that we could share. He wanted to know what I liked most on the menu. I told him just to choose his favorites this time, and he did. They were all my favorites, enchiladas, tacos, and tamales. It's as if he could read my mind. We talked and laughed until the restaurant closed. He was such a great conversationalist.

"What is New York like?" I asked.

"Well, it is an island, so coming inland, you always have to cross a bridge. We lived in an apartment above the restaurant, so I rarely went inland, except to visit my mom's parents before they died. They lived in White Plains, New York, which was about 45 minutes from where my dad and I lived. It's humid there in the summer and cold in the winter. We get a lot of rain. I lived in Manhattan and frequented Central Park in the summertime. My dad and I used to give out expired bread to the homeless people at Central Park. I admired my dad for his warm heart. He was a large man who most people would say looked rough, but he was a teddy bear, always thinking about others."

"I wish I had had the pleasure of knowing your dad. He sounds just like you." I responded as my heart raced.

"He would have adored you, and he would have wanted you to teach him how to bake all your delicious pies," He said.

He continued, "He'd say, Teddy, you did good son!"

Even though he would say that to his son, I was the one who felt blessed. Maybe all those prayers had finally been answered. I had met my John Travolta who made me feel like more than a woman. I know it all sounds corny, but when you meet the one who makes you smile and have waited all of your life, it is well worth the lonely nights. Ted was the one.

"We are too late for dessert." He said on our drive back to my apartment.

"Rain check?" I asked.

"Yes, rain check." He repeated. "Mary Grace, meeting you has been so great. I think we should consider becoming business partners and opening a bakery or a restaurant together."

"Well, Ted, meeting you has been a pleasure, but we just met. What if we are not good business partners?" I asked.

"Look, I have never met a woman who I can talk to for hours, someone who likes to cook and bake as much as me, and another human being who makes me feel happy. Isn't that enough? Don't you believe in love at first sight?" He asked.

"I guess I do." I said.

I felt something very special for Ted, and even though I hardly knew him, it was as if I had known him all my life. Maybe God had brought us together, as I remembered the prayers Tim and I had prayed, to one day know when we met our perfect match. I had written a list of what I wanted in a man, prayed over it, and now I was already falling in love with a man I had just met who matched all the criteria, except for the fact that he wasn't John Travolta. Some things cannot be explained or reasoned. They just happen. When I hugged Ted good night, I could hear his heart beat. I looked into his eyes, and he kissed me, a kiss that felt so good that you never want him to stop. He did stop because he knew I was a good Christian girl. Besides, he was a good Christian guy! Sometimes I wished I wasn't so obedient, and this was one of those times. I knew doing it God's way was the best way, as Tim would remind me.

"Not only a hint of sexual immorality." I could hear Tim saying to me.

The thing is I knew God made himself known, that he answers prayers. One day Ted and I wouldn't stop, after we were married, of course. I had met the man of my dreams.

CHAPTER

18

He belongs to me and I to him.

I promise to love you, to cherish you, to make memories with you, so if we depart, you will never be that far away from me. The memories we make together are enough to sustain me through life.

Ted and I opened a bakery/restaurant together and named it *A Piece of Heaven*, to honor my friend, Nevaeh. She was so delighted and was even more excited when I asked her if I could put her picture on the wall of our restaurant and in the menus, with her story about the healing basket. We drove her many times to Albuquerque, New Mexico, to help us with the bakery in our restaurant. She made tortillas and blueberry muffins every time she came because they were easy for her.

After running the bakery/restaurant for several years, Ted and I had a small wedding one weekend. Of course, our wedding caused so much chaos with our families, but Nevaeh said we did the right thing because we were thinking with our hearts. We began confiding in Tim, who said that it's better to marry than to burn with passion. Tim agreed to officiate our marriage as long as we stayed pure. We waited until our wedding night before having sex, but we also had to deal with our passion. Sure, we were in love and in certain moments, sometimes we have to go with love and take a chance, but we didn't want to plan an elaborate wedding, just to disappoint God in case we couldn't wait. Our marriage was still beautiful, and we were happy. I had seen people who had large expensive weddings and ended up so unhappy and depressed. Our marriage cost us under $1,000.00, and we honeymooned at one of his uncle's cabins further north. It was perfect. That's all that mattered to us.

After our marriage, Tim became so busy that I hardly saw him anymore, but he would call me at least once a week. He was enjoying his ministry and had built a great friendship with Pastor Salas.

"I haven't had any seizures, and everyone in my congregation is praying for me." Tim told me when Ted and I returned from our honeymoon.

He continued, "I want you to know that Hope has moved back to our community, and her sister Rachel is currently in Mexico on a mission trip. Hope and I are dating, well, sort of. She doesn't judge me and isn't afraid of my seizures."

"There is nothing to judge, my friend. You are a great guy. I love you and keep you in my prayers. Hope is everything you asked God for, so she's the one."

"I miss you, Mary Grace. You are correct. Our prayers are being answered. It's in God's timing." He paused. "Oh, and can you send up some more baked goods with Nevaeh?" He asked.

"You just miss my baking, Tim." I said laughing.

"Well, I miss that too but I have no one to laugh at my jokes anymore, so of course I notice your absence. Send me some jelly with the bread." He said, giggling.

"Please give Hope my best." I said.

"She remembers you, and your paintings of the rainbows. I told her those rainbows are her light. We talk quite a bit, but she isn't ready for a relationship, just a friendship. I might still die a virgin."

"You won't. She really seems to care about you, Tim. Besides, you are so loveable. Prayers are so powerful, and this is great news! I'd like to see her when we're in town," I replied. "I will send those cannolis that you and the other pastors like so much, some fresh baked bread, jelly, and apple pies. I will also send tortillas, and Ted is sending you some green chili."

"Thank you. Hope is very beautiful, Mary Grace, and we get together and pray several days a week. I think she still needs time, after everything she's been through. Give Ted my best and thank him for me. We love his baked goods. Talk to you again soon. Adios, my friend." Tim replied and hung up the phone before I could say good-bye.

He didn't like good-bye, so he always said Adios, which meant 'Go with God.' Tim was doing so well, and I was so happy for him. People who were mean to us in high school were now treating us with respect. What was important to Tim was the fact that he was building a relationship with our community. People had apologized to him for making fun of him, and he chose forgiveness over hate. Sometimes Tim saw Sarah at church. She had been in sobriety for two years and was attending a program at the church Tim led. I continued to pray for her, and I was always giving God thanks for all of the miracles only he could do! All we have to do is pray…and believe that our prayers will be answered.

Ted and I were busier than usual after our short honeymoon. Even though our families were unhappy about our tiny wedding, Nevaeh approved of every decision we made because, like she reminded us almost every time we brought it up, we have to live with the consequences. No one else has to live with the cost of our choices, both good and bad, so as long as we could sleep at night, she would tell us, we can live with what we decide. Besides, God isn't going to ask us about other people, just about our own decisions. Nevaeh had been working making tortillas and muffins all morning on this particular visit. Our tortillas tasted similar, but hers were perfectly round. I tried to make mine round, but they were never as round as hers.

"I could make these in my sleep," Nevaeh would say about her tortillas. "As long as I had flour."

"The health department would shut us down if you did make tortillas in your sleep." Ted would tease her.

We would laugh because we imagined flour in her bed while she made tortillas. She walked around the restaurant and met the patrons. They were delighted to meet the woman who had inspired us, and she always found a way to sell out of everything she made.

"Nevaeh!" Ted would jokingly say, "We want you to sell all the baked goods, even the cannolis ! Not just the tortillas and blueberry muffins, my dear."

She would touch his face and respond, "Now, is it my fault that I'm better at baking than you? I did teach the best of the best, and you married her. May I remind you she beat you in that baking contest, fair and square?"

He would laugh and say, in his New York accent, "Yeah, yeah, yeah."

As I listened to them speak, I thought about all the memories we were making. It broke my heart to think that one day Nevaeh would no longer be with us. Then, it dawned on me that Ted and I could pass away suddenly. There were no guarantees in life, so this is why memories, good memories, should always be made.

Some days I felt so stressed out, with the business and the money we were making. We were making a lot of money. Ted insisted we buy a van, in case we had to deliver our cakes, which took off. We were making birthday cakes, wedding cakes, and cakes for all occasions. I kept mementoes in my healing basket, although I kept my basket at my parent's house, so I put them in a box and transported them every time I went home. I kept letters that customers wrote to us, our first his and her aprons, and our pencil drawing of our bakery/restaurant, which was pretty close to the final draft. We additionally had a website, which was holding at a 4.8 out of 5 stars, with over 600 reviews. We had also received rave reviews from the Journal, and we had been featured in a local magazine. Many people said the name of our business matched our baked goods, which, as they wrote, were "heavenly." I placed all of the customer letters and some of the online reviews and the features from the magazine in my healing basket. One day, I thought, I could share these memories with our children and grandchildren.

I counted my blessings, and I was in such a great place in my life, but this made me feel so guilty because life was so hard for many of my friends and family. I'm not saying life wasn't hard for me, but I had a way of dealing with the stress and the disappointments. I knew how to cope with grief. I knew grief wasn't just about losing a loved one. It was also about losing your best friend or dealing with trage-dies in your community and in your own family units. It was about acceptance of your friends who had seizures and not believing other people's opinions.

I had been put through so much in my life but chose to take a different path, and I had Nevaeh to thank. She had a way of think-ing about things and dealing with tragedies. When I got down and depressed, I remembered how Nevaeh dealt with her sadness. So many people choose drugs and alcohol, and although I'm not judging them for their choices, things could be different for them if they found other outlets. Even I had a tendency to choose unhealthy orifices.

For me, I occasionally used food as a coping skill, but instead of eating my sorrow away, Nevaeh taught me to bake it and give it away, or in this case, sell it to make a living. Baking and cooking was a way of dealing with my grief, and if I chose to stuff my feelings, which sometimes I did, I would eat some of my food. However, most of the time, I sold my food to people who enjoyed it, not as an unhealthy coping skill, but because everyone has to eat, and we were doing something positive for our community. I think this is why Ted and I got along so well. We both loved food, and we were productive in the way we used food. We had learned to make a living with something that could potentially be unhealthy for us.

We made great memories for people who were having birthday parties or were getting married. This was productive, and it kept me remembering Nevaeh and all the wonderful things she taught me growing up. She showed me a way to live that can only bring good things to my life. If something tragic happened, I knew how to deal with it. I'd write a letter or bake cookies to give away or share stories with my customers. People kept coming back to our bakery/restau-rant. They talked to us about their losses. Sometimes we felt like we were professional bakery therapists, but people felt comfortable opening up to us.

It made me realize how lonely people felt. Some of our elderly regulars didn't have places to go for the Holidays, so we started a 50 and over Christmas night. We'd host a party for our guests one week before Christmas. Many of our patrons were grateful for this get together. Ted would buy presents and wrap them, and some of our customers told us they had not received a gift in years.

Nevaeh became the guest of honor for these festivities. Some of the viejitos, old men, tried to get her attention by buying her gifts and writing her "love letters." She was always flattered, but she would make it clear that she wasn't looking for a husband. Watching her with these men was so much fun! I think she secretly wanted to take some of these men home with her, but by the end of the night, she would come down to earth and tell us she was just making good memories.

"There were two rules in my household." Nevaeh said more than once, "One is to seek God with all your heart and the second one is to make good memories. So, actually, I'm not flirting with these men. I'm just making good memories."

She was such a cutie pie! I still thought she was flirting, but what did I know? I had one best friend, Tim, who talked about purity constantly, and a husband, the only man I had every really dated or had an intimate relationship with. So, maybe she was just being nice.

The memories we made with Nevaeh are etched in my mind and every time I think about her, like she once told me, I would thank God. I put her rules to practice because they just made sense. They would stay with me for the rest of my life.

LAST CHAPTER

In life and in death, we belong to the Lord.

When I read your letter, I see your face, I hear
your voice, and I know you are close by. Your
stories will always give me hope, faith, courage,
and truth. You are my forever friend. I love you.

I continued to visit Nevaeh for many years after I moved away. Things were somewhat different, however, because I knew she grieved sometimes without me, but she made it clear that she did not mind. When we could, we lamented together. She still baked bread every time I saw her, and she washed vegetables during the summer months for me to take after our visits. Ted fit into our friendship perfectly. He danced with both of us, and sometimes when we listened to the *Saturday Night Fever* album, he would walk across her living room while the song *Staying Alive* played on the old turn table. He would move his rear end like John Travolta, and Nevaeh and I would whistle and laugh until we cried tears of joy. Then we would wait for the next song, *More than a Woman*, and he would take us into his arms, one person at a time. He was such a good dancer, but of course, in my eyes, he was good at everything.

Each time Ted and I would visit Nevaeh, she said he was great, and he always brought her a special treat that he made. She enjoyed his cannolis, his French bread, his spaghetti, and especially his lasagna. He offered to teach her how to make them, but she appreciated him preparing them for her. As she grew older, she cooked and baked less and less. Ted would make one of his special dishes in her kitchen while she and I visited in the living room. He preserved our friendship all he could because he knew I needed her, and she was growing old.

We ate his great creations and laughed at the dinner table. She told Ted he was a much better dancer than my childhood crush, John Travolta. However, we never saw John Travolta dance. We just imagined his dance moves by the picture on the record album. Ted would smile with his big blue eyes admiring our best friend.

There were always great memories I made with Nevaeh. We continued to make them with Ted, while we dated and after we got married. She was kind and gentle to both of us. She had so much wisdom and insight. She accepted me as I grew up and never judged me. If she ever hurt my feelings, I can't remember because she strived to make me smile and she was truly my friend, a companion who taught me to grieve with healthy coping strategies. She introduced me to the kitchen and taught me to deal with sadness through the stories brought about from a healing basket.

"I owe you." Ted would say to Nevaeh. "You taught my wife how to deal with life in such a positive way. She always talks about you fondly. I have *two* women to love now."

She often told me she had a crush on Ted, but he had one on her too. I didn't mind because they were both amazing human beings. Besides, their crushes were innocent and out in the open. I was never jealous of the love they had for one another, and isn't life all about love anyway?

After she died on an unusually warm October day, and in the months following her funeral, her daughter dropped off a letter for me at my parents' house. I was living in a suburb near Albuquerque, New Mexico with Ted. Neither of us were ready for children because we were working so many hours, but we wanted to have them before

Nevaeh died. We didn't reach this goal. We were running a business, which became very lucrative and busy, especially before the Holidays.

At our last 50 and over Christmas party, all of Nevaeh's friends were melancholy. We missed her. Emptiness filled the bakery that December day and for the week following the gathering.

Before driving back home to see my family, we had to clean the bakery kitchen and it seemed to take longer during the winter months. People came in and out of our bakery and we had lines of people waiting for cookies and cakes. We barely had time to sit down and rest, but we enjoyed our business, and we worked together, which we treasured.

We got a late start to my parent's house on Christmas Eve the year she died. The next day, Christmas Day, I received the letter that Nevaeh wrote me, after my mom remembered she had put it away for me. My mom said she had forgotten to tell me she left it in my healing basket, and Lily told my mom that I was to read it as a tribute to an old friend. Nevaeh had written it a few months before she died from the cancer that ravaged her body. The letter was in a big envelope, I noticed, as I sat down on the living room couch, where I could see the snow falling outside the large front window. I remembered Nevaeh telling me how she was afraid of the snow in New Hampshire, but she had taught me how to be brave, just like her dad made her courageous when he went away to Normandy. No snow storm or war could ever bring back the demons. They were gone forever. As I read through her words, I could not hold back the tears, but I knew crying was a good coping skill, since I had done it numerous times for many years with my friend. She reminisced about our various visits. She wrote about when I learned to bake bread and pies. She confessed that at first, she was afraid to taste my baked goods but realized I had a natural ability to bake. I smiled as tears rolled down my face. She had such a great sense of humor. I remembered when she told me that Jesus snored, and now I really knew the truth about how she was afraid to taste my early baking.

She valued when we washed dishes and talked. She wrote about dancing with me in the living room and my being in love with John Travolta. She re-told some of the stories in her healing basket and asked me to remember them. I could not forget the many stories she had shared with me.

"You can still remember and grieve with me because in each story is a memory of us." She wrote.

She mentioned the day I had discovered her mourning, and she thanked me for sharing in her grief. She was so happy to have found a little friend who grew up to be such a beautiful woman. She was so proud of me for making my own healing basket and knew it would help me grow emotionally and spiritually. She told me not to be afraid of the unknown, and to always keep my heart open and kind. She wrote in her letter I was medicine to her soul. I wondered if she knew the profound impact she had on my life. She must know now, I believed.

She told me she thought that Ted was my match. In the letter, she said everyone meets their soulmate sometime in life, but many have lost them because of stupidity. She said we all make mistakes when we are young, and like everyone else, including her, I probably made my share of mistakes too. However, when it came to finding the right man, I hit the jackpot.

"If you hadn't found him first," she wrote, "I would have taken him for myself. Wink. Wink."

Of course, she was just being Neveah because she knew I would be crying at this very moment, so she wanted to make me giggle. I wiped my tears and then I laughed.

I picked up the envelope and noticed there was something else inside. On the bottom of the envelope were pressed lilies. I continued to allow the tears to drop, and to smile at some of her thoughts in the letter. I felt at peace, knowing that she was reunited with her parents, and I imagined her embracing them. I could see their faces in my mind, like the ones in her pictures. Her dad was wearing his uniform, finding out that he had earned a Purple Heart, but it was more rewarding to finally be reunited with the little girl he left behind, seeing a woman with much wisdom and discernment that would make any father proud. Nevaeh's mom would be holding a beautiful bouquet of lilies. In my mind, I could see that her parents had the biggest smiles than any of the other angels in heaven. I imagined her son, Estevan, who also greeted her with a big smile, just like the one in the picture. I wondered if he was still a child or if he had become a man. In my mind, I pretended that he was putting his arms around Nevaeh like Tim often did. He was the best hugger in heaven. I just knew it. There, Nevaeh would find that the pain, sorrow, and tears we had so often shared were nonexistent. In paradise, she would feel no fear. In paradise, she would only find joy. In paradise, she would find healing for the very soul that had found its purpose and itself. Nevaeh would see the lilies surrounding her, preparing a way for her daughter and her grandchildren, for me, for Tim and Ted, and for everyone whose lives she had touched. The anchor of hope kept her ship afloat, and once again, I could see her face in my mind and hear her voice in my heart. My amazing friend had finally found her peace in heaven. She had made her way home, above the clouds and away from the snow, where evil could not exist. She was walking on pure gold, as pure as the soul that had inspired me, loved me, and given me the strength to continue my journey in this world. Somehow, I secretly knew she wasn't so far away.

She must have been close to me that Christmas Day. I felt her by my side and *heard* her voice because at the end of her letter, she wrote, "Remember, when you are sad or there are storms around you, look and you will see heaven. Heaven is a matter of perspective. Heaven is our strength when we are weak. Heaven is our joy when we are sad. Heaven is our light when there is darkness. Heaven, my beautiful Mary Grace, is within us. ~Nevaeh."

The past memories flashed in my head like an old movie. Nevaeh had shown me how to cope with what sometimes felt like hell, all of the bad things and the sad things in our lives, so that we could enjoy glimpses of heaven on earth. She succeeded. I could live the rest of my life seeking God with all of my heart and making good memories. This was her legacy to me, and her gifts, all the wonderful mementoes in her healing basket, would never die. The stories she shared with me about the treasures in her basket remained with me for always. God had blessed me with a beautiful friend. I once read a scripture that said to show hospitality to strangers because by doing so, you might be entertaining angels. Nevaeh may not have been a stranger to me, but she was my guardian angel—God knew her by name. He had called her home.

I instinctively turned the envelope around and read a scripture she had written down, Luke 20:36: "and they can no longer die, for they are like angels…"

Indeed! She was my saving grace, a reflection of heaven on earth.

DONATIONS

"A portion of the author's royalties will be donated to the Children's Grief Center of New Mexico, which provides special support services for children, teens, young adults (ages 5-25) and their caregivers after the death of a loved one. Please send any additional donations to https://childrensgrief.org/donate/, or call 505-323-0478; and also to the Grief Resource Center located in Albuquerque, New Mexico— 'lighting the pathways to healing'— offering free support for adults over the age of 18. Donations can be directly sent to https://www.griefnm.org/about/donate-to-the-grief-resource-center/, or call 505-842-7166."

ABOUT THE AUTHOR

*C*larissa Rudolph-Hastings is one of the 2018 Ambassadors of the Word for the United States of America, as appointed by the Cesar Egido Serrano Foundation, an organization in Toledo, Spain, that promotes international peace and unity through dialogue. Her writing is influenced from her experiences as a counselor, teacher, and scientist. As a teacher, she has worked with Sandia National Laboratories and Intel to bring microtechnology, biotechnology, and project-based learning into the classroom, a task she has executed with a great deal of success to her students. She was nominated as the Golden Apple Teacher of the Year Award and the National Biology Teacher of the Year Award in 2004. She has volunteered her time as a Regional Science Fair Judge at New Mexico Highlands University in Las Vegas, New Mexico, over the last two years. Since completing her Master of Arts Degree in 1998, Clarissa has worked as a counselor, both in a treatment center and in public schools. This year, she was nominated as one of the 2017-2018 Counselors of Year Awards for an elementary school. She has additionally gained experience as a Chaplain, which opened her eyes to how people deal with death. Her ideas as a writer on the topic of grief, however, stem mostly from her personal experience of losing her parents so young. She believes that sorrow is a lifetime occurrence that is a part of our journey. Her strength comes from her relationship with God, who gives her the tools and strategies to cope with pain through tears, prayer, and reading the Bible. Currently, she is collaborating with other Ambassadors throughout the world to write an Anthology for Peace, which is upcoming.

21822312R00075

Made in the USA
San Bernardino, CA
05 January 2019